COMPLETE
CAT CARE
MANUAL

COMPLETE CAT CARE MANUAL

ANDREW EDNEY, B.V.M., M.R.C.V.S.

Foreword by Roger Caras,
President, ASPCA

DORLING KINDERSLEY
LONDON • NEW YORK • STUTTGART

A DORLING KINDERSLEY BOOK

Project Editor

Alison Melvin

Art Editor

Lee Griffiths

Managing Editor

Krystyna Mayer

Managing Art Editor

Derek Coombes

Photographers

Steve Gorton • Tim Ridley

Production Controller

Antony Heller

U.S. Editor

Mary Ann Lynch

ASPCA Consultant

Stephen Zawistowski, Ph.D.

Foreword by Roger Caras, President, ASPCA

First American Edition, 1992

10 9 8 7 6 5 4 3

Published in the United States by Dorling Kindersley Inc.,
95 Madison Avenue,
New York, New York 10016

Distributed by Houghton Mifflin Company, Boston.

Edney, A. T. B.
    ASPCA Complete Cat Care Manual: the ultimate
illustrated guide to caring for your cat / by Andrew
Edney: photographs by Steve Gorton and Tim Ridley.—
1st American ed.
        p. cm.
    Includes index.
    ISBN 1-56458-064-4
    1. Cats. 2. Cats — Health. I. Gorton, Steve. II.
Ridley, Tim. III. Title.
SF447.E36 1992
636.8 — dc20   92-52783
                                                        CIP

Reproduced by Pica, Singapore
Printed and bound in Italy by Arnoldo Mondadori Editore, Italy

CONTENTS

THE ASPCA AND CAT CARE

NO ONE IS sure why cats purr, except that it seems, in part at least, to be one way of showing that they feel very strongly about us. We do not fully understand what constitutes intensity in a cat's mind, or even how, what, and to what degree cats think; but they do think – that much has been determined – and we'd like to believe that they think good things about us. They certainly purr when they are around us. They apparently like us as much as we like them.

The affection and respect for animals that many people share resulted in the formation of the The American Society for the Prevention of Cruelty to Animals in 1866. It is the Western Hemisphere's oldest humane society, whose purpose, as stated by its founder, Henry Bergh, is "to provide effective means for the prevention of cruelty to animals throughout the United States."

Bergh's initial efforts on behalf of animals struck a resonant cord throughout the country. Within five years, additional SPCAs could be found from coast to coast. Each of these SPCAs was a separate, individual society, formed to meet the needs of its own community. While they were not directly connected with Bergh's ASPCA, they did share his commitment and goals, and still frequently rely on the APSCA for guidance and advice.

Today, more than 125 years later, the ASPCA continues its work by operating shelters and an animal hospital in New York City. Authorized as peace officers, its Humane Law Enforcement agents continue Bergh's work by investigating instances of cruelty to animals. The ASPCA's educational and legislative programs reach millions of people across the country each year.

Many of the problems that all humane societies across the country are forced to deal with are the result of uncaring, irresponsible, or simply poorly informed pet owners. Education plays an integral role in correcting and preventing these problems by providing people with the information they need to care for their companion animals in a humane and responsible fashion.

Cats now outnumber dogs – they are the most popular pets in America, living in over 30 percent of households. Unfortunately, not every cat has the good fortune of living with a caring, knowledgeable owner.

Each year, millions of cats die as a result of neglect, cruelty, for want of good homes, and sometimes simply through ignorance. This book contains valuable information that everyone sharing a home with a cat can use to provide the best care possible for his pet. Such information can only result in good things for your cat, and for you, as you enrich each other's lives.

As you will learn, cats have been domesticated for roughly 4,000 years. Over these many centuries cats have fared quite differently in many cultures. The Egyptians, the first people to live with cats, came to worship them. During the Middle Ages, Europeans blamed them for evil and tied them into witchcraft and other strange beliefs. Thankfully, cats today are valued for themselves and the wonderful companions they make. This no doubt helps to account for their ever-increasing popularity around the world.

Sometimes we can have too much of a good thing. Right now there are many more cats being born every day than there are good homes available. Remember that spaying or neutering your pet will not only help to ensure that all cats have a chance to find a good home, but will help to keep your cat healthier and happier for years to come.

Enjoy those years of companionship, because they will certainly be special for both of you.

Roger Caras
President
American Society for the Prevention
of Cruelty to Animals

INTRODUCTION

IT IS ONLY during the last few thousand years that the cat has become domesticated, developing from small, wild ancestors that first roamed the Earth about 12 million years ago. Even before then, the larger cats, such as lions, tigers, and leopards, were developing from a few prototypes, while other members of the cat family branched in a different direction to become specialist hunters like the cheetah, or small, forest-dwelling felines like the ocelot and the margay.

As people moved around the world, the cat went with them. The earliest signs of domestication were probably seen in the Middle East. The Ancient Egyptians were the first civilization to realize the cat's potential as a vermin hunter, that protected the grain supplies on which their lives depended. It is not surprising, then, that this reliance turned to worship. The cat became a deity in Ancient Egypt and was almost as well loved as it is today. Although it is not regarded as a deity anymore, worship has been replaced with a caring, loving relationship with presentday owners.

Having enjoyed many years of great favor, it was perhaps inevitable that fortune should turn against the cat for a black period in its history. In the fifteenth and sixteenth centuries, human ignorance and bigotry were directed at anything that could be blamed for the world's ills, and, just as the Ancient Egyptians looked upon the cat as an expression of divinity, religious groups in Europe encouraged a phase of hatred and fear, resulting in the cat being seen as an agent of the devil. This period eventually passed, however, and the elegance, beauty, engaging personality, and inestimable value of the cat as a companion were finally recognized. It is now one of the most popular pets in the world.

Essential Care

Deciding to add a cat to your household should not be taken lightly if you and your pet are to be happy together. Therefore, it is essential that you know exactly how to care for a cat; from choosing a healthy kitten, to reproduction, house training, and basic discipline. A major section of this book covers all the varied aspects of day-to-day cat care. Becoming a cat owner is a serious business, and this chapter gives advice on what to look for when adopting or purchasing your pet, basic equipment such as cat collars and baskets, and containers for traveling with your pet.

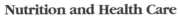

Nutrition and Health Care

A cat is a carnivore with very specific nutritional needs, and the information in this book makes the basics of its dietary and medicinal requirements as comprehensive and as readable as possible. All cat owners need some guidance on how to recognize health problems with their pets and what action to take when something is not right. The extensive health care section of this manual deals with everyday problems such as ear mites, worms, and fleas, as well as first aid in emergencies and treatment of serious illnesses. There is also a diagnosis chart, so you can quickly find the cause of your pet's problem and the appropriate treatment. Owners are also advised how to nurse a sick cat, so that it recovers quickly and without stress. In all cases, owners are urged to consult their local veterinary practice for help and guidance. Reproduction is extensively covered in a special section, with advice on planning a litter, helping your cat give birth, and caring for young kittens. There is even information on how different genes are passed on to give your pet certain characteristics, and first aid for your cat in the event of any problems both during and after giving birth, or if the kittens are sickly.

Showing Your Cat

You may want to enter your cat in shows, and this book explains all you need to know about preparing for competition. Even if you do not, grooming is still an essential part of everyday feline care, especially for longhaired cats. The chapter on grooming describes how various types of feline coat should be groomed, and how to bathe your pet and care for its teeth and claws. Special grooming for a cat show is also included, along with information on how a pedigree cat is judged

Finding Out More

The glossary explains the specialized feline terms used in the book. Finally, there is a short section providing information on the various feline organizations, as well as suggestions for further reading. Once you begin learning about your cat, you might never want to stop!

Chapter 1

INTRODUCING THE CAT

CATS ARE always enigmatic and enchanting, and they have been a source of fascination for mankind throughout history. The cat has been worshiped and persecuted in turn, but it is now in the ascendant again. Cats are perfectly suited to the urban lifestyle of twentieth-century society. Whether pedigree or ordinary housecat, they make attractive, rewarding, and relatively easy-to-care-for pets. Indispensable companions to people of all ages and nationalities, they are chameleon characters; fearless hunters one moment, and purring comforters the next.

THE FIRST DOMESTIC CATS

ORIGINS OF THE DOMESTIC CAT

Even though its ancestors walked the Earth over 12 million years ago, it has only been about 4,000 years since the cat was domesticated. The Ancient Egyptians first used cats to control vermin in their grain stores, but there is evidence of wild cats sharing human caves and villages long before that.

In Egypt, the cat was revered as a hunter, and it became deified as an incarnation of the goddess Bastet. Other ancient civilizations later began to domesticate the cat, and Phoenician traders took tame felines to Italy; from there they spread slowly across Europe. Eventually, they even migrated to the New World with the Pilgrims. Despite a period of persecution in the Middle Ages, when cats were associated with the devil, by the eighteenth century cats had become popular as household pets and had spread all over the world.

Vermin hunter
A 13th century manuscript shows cats in their traditional role as killers of vermin. The first domestic cats had to earn their keep by destroying pests to protect stores of food.

Cat goddess
A bronze statue of the Egyptian cat goddess Bastet, from around 600 BC.

Good against evil
An Egyptian wall painting dating from around 1500 BC shows the sun god Ra as a cat, slaying Apep, the serpent of darkness.

Eastern feline (above)
The domestic cat probably reached India before spreading to China or Japan. This Indian painting dates from around 1810.

ANCESTORS OF THE DOMESTIC CAT

The cats we know today, from lions and tigers to household pets, are descended from early carnivores called the miacids, which evolved from the first carnivorous mammals, the creodonts. While some miacids became lions, tigers, and cheetahs, Martelli's wild cat (*Felis lunensis*) is thought to have been a direct ancestor of all modern small cats. It gave rise to the modern wild cat (*Felis sylvestris*), which developed into three main types: the European wild cat, the African wild cat, and the Asiatic desert cat. The domestic cat (*Felis catus*) is thought to have evolved from the African wild cat.

African wild cat
The African wild cat is the most likely ancestor of the domestic cat. It has tabby markings.

European wild cat
This may have added genes to the domestic cat by interbreeding.

Jungle cat *(left)*
Kept in Ancient Egypt, but probably not related to modern cats.

THE SPREAD OF THE DOMESTIC CAT

1970s *Japanese Bobtail reaches the United States from Japan*

Late 19th century *Longhaired cats reach United States from Great Britain*

Mid-19th century *Longhaired cats reach Great Britain from Turkey*

AD 4 *Shorthaired cats spread across Europe from Italy, reaching Great Britain in AD 900*

16th century *Longhaired cats taken to Italy from Turkey*

Circa 900 BC *Shorthaired cats taken to Italy from Egypt*

17th century *Shorthaired cats taken to United States by first settlers*

1930s *Burmese taken to United States from Burma*

Late 19th century *Abyssinians reach Great Britain from Abyssinia*

Late 19th century *Siamese reaches Great Britain from Thailand*

1950s *Korat reaches United States from Thailand*

16th century *Manx cats taken to Isle of Man from the Far East*

1970s *Singapura taken to United States from Singapore*

Process of domestication
The shorthaired domestic cat spread across the world from Egypt, while longhaired cats came much later from Turkey, Iran, and Afghanistan.

THE FELINE SENSES

The senses of the domestic cat, like those of its wild relatives, are designed for the purpose of stalking and killing prey. Its sense organs are those of a predator, and it can detect the slightest movement and the faintest sound. A cat's hearing, sight, touch, and smell are far more acute than in humans and most other mammals. It can see in the dimmest of lights; it can detect very high-pitched noises; and it can even taste certain smells by using the Jacobson's organ in the roof of its mouth. A cat is highly sensitive to its surroundings and will thrive under the right conditions, but it may not do so well in a home where its needs are not met. Shy cats and children often do not mix; loud noises and sudden movements can be frightening.

THE FIVE SENSES

The mouth and taste
A cat has a discriminating sense of taste. Giving a cat medicine by mixing it with its food can prove difficult, since a cat can usually detect any additions to its food bowl. Unlike dogs, cats do not have a sweet tooth, but some pampered pets do develop a liking for cake and fruit.

The ears and hearing
A cat's hearing is very acute, and it can hear high-frequency sounds up to two octaves higher than a human. A cat can usually be trained to recognize and respond to certain words, such as its name, by the tone of voice used.

The whiskers and touch
The whiskers act as antennae and help a cat avoid objects in dim light. A cat is extremely sensitive to touch, and each individual hair on its body is responsive to the slightest vibration in its environment.

The nose and smell

All cats are territorial and mark their territory with scent to warn off other felines. A cat's sense of smell is enhanced by the Jacobson's organ, which enables a cat to analyze intriguing scents by tasting the molecules on the back of its tongue. This is called "flehming."

The eyes and sight

Although a cat has poor color vision, its eyes are designed to make use of any available light so that it can see in extremely dim conditions. Its sight is that of a hunter, and it possesses a far wider angle of view than a human, which allows it to detect tiny movements of prey animals.

CATS AND CATNIP

The smell of catnip or catmint *(Nepeta cataria)* is irresistible to most, but not all, cats. Many cats react to the plant by sniffing it, rubbing their heads in it, rolling around in a trancelike state on their backs, and purring loudly. The effects of catnip are shortlived, and it is not thought to be addictive or to cause any unpleasant aftereffects. Another plant, valerian, produces similar effects.

Sniffing catnip *(left)*
A cat sniffs the scent of dried catnip for a few seconds before it takes effect. Some cats are not susceptible to the plant and may show no visible signs.

Typical behavior
More than 50 percent of cats respond to catnip by getting very excited and rolling around ecstatically.

MOVEMENT AND BALANCE

The cat is a hunter and predator and needs to be quick on its feet and extremely agile. Its body is specifically designed for maximum speed from minimum effort. Most of the time a cat conserves its energy, but when it needs to, it is capable of sprinting very fast. A cat can travel at a top speed of approximately 30 miles (48 km) per hour over a short distance, enabling it to pounce on its prey before it can escape. Whereas most animals have to spend much of their lives on the ground, a cat has enviable coordination for climbing, jumping, and balancing.

FELINE COORDINATION

Jumping

All cats are superb athletes and can perform an amazing repertoire of vertical, horizontal, and twisting leaps. A cat can jump up to five times its own height in a single bound. Its strong hind-leg muscles and flexible spine enable it to thrust itself into the air and land again safely without injuring itself. A cat will always look before it leaps, carefully assessing the distance before taking off.

The tail maintains perfect balance

The cat's claws are ready to push off from the tree

Balancing

A cat is extremely well coordinated because it possesses a very efficient system for sending messages to the brain from its muscles and joints. It uses its tail as a counterbalance when walking along a narrow branch, in the same way as a tightrope walker holds a long pole for balance.

The eyes are fixed straight ahead

The claws grip the branch

Climbing

From a tree or fence, a cat can patrol its territory and watch its prey without being seen. Using its strong hind-leg muscles and gripping with its front claws, going up is relatively easy, but coming down can be more difficult.

THE RIGHTING REFLEX

The eyes survey the ground

The paws are positioned on a narrow branch

The hind legs are carefully balanced

Turning over

A cat's balance and coordination are unsurpassed, and this has led to the belief that a cat is able to withstand a fall from a great height. This is not always the case, but some cats have survived falls of over 65 ft (20 meters). The cat's righting reflex works automatically and quickly. The cat's eyes and balance organs in the inner ear tell it where it is in space, and it lands on its feet.

ASSESSING A CAT'S MOOD

Your cat lets you know when it is pleased, angry, frightened, or unhappy. Eyes, ears, tail, whiskers, and voice are all powerful indicators of your pet's mood. Although sometimes regarded as lone hunters, cats are very sociable animals that have evolved a complex body language and a range of different vocal sounds to communicate with you and with other felines. A cat's face is particularly telling, expressing a variety of different emotions ranging from contentment to fear and aggression.

BODY LANGUAGE

Happy Cat
Your cat may greet you with its tail held high and the tail tip bent slightly forward. An erect tail indicates that a cat is happy and confident. A tail flicked from side to side indicates a state of tension. A cat on the defensive fluffs up its coat and its tail fur in order to appear larger.

The tail is erect and held stiffly

Alert expression with ears pricked forward

First meeting
Cats usually establish their social order without incurring serious injury. Intense staring and emphatic body language may deter more timid cats. The engagement may break up with each cat washing itself in a very deliberate way.

Aggressive cat
A cat lying on its back is not necessarily submitting to a more dominant feline. With its teeth and claws showing, a formidable array of weaponry is displayed.

The ears are flattened against the head

Defensive cat
A cat poised to make a strategic withdrawal may remain still for several minutes. The attention is focused, the gaze intense, and the ears pricked forward to monitor any sound.

Close companions

Cats that are part of the same household will greet each other affectionately by touching noses and rubbing their bodies together. Cats that are best friends will groom each other, sleep huddled together, and play with one another.

Cat calls

The vocal repertoire of a cat is extensive, with more than 16 different sounds. Cat calls include howls of anger, yowls and growls of tomcats fighting, as well as queens in heat looking for mates. According to the intonation, a cat's meow can be used to express many different moods.

Making contact

Rubbing against people is an endearing habit, but your cat is not simply being affectionate. It is marking out territory with the secretions of glands around its face. The tail area and paws also carry the cat's scent.

A cat marks its territory by rubbing against objects

PURRING

The purr is a low-frequency sound that is produced not by the vocal chords but from somewhere deep in a cat's chest. Purring is usually a sign of pleasure or contentment. A mother cat purrs when her kittens are born and when they begin to suckle; tiny kittens purr when they feel secure, warm, and well fed. However, a cat will also purr to comfort itself when it is nervous or in pain.

Purring for pleasure
Purring is a uniquely feline sound that usually means that a cat is relaxed and contented.

THE CAT AS A PET

Cats are becoming ever more popular household pets worldwide. There are at present about 100 million cats in the Western world *(see opposite)* and the numbers are on the increase. There are many reasons for this immense feline popularity. For example, cats require a lot less time and expense than many other pets and are particularly well suited to living in an urban environment. They are independent, inexpensive to purchase and to maintain, very clean, and they keep mice and other vermin out of the home. Cats are also very affectionate and make extremely devoted friends, especially for older people, or for someone who lives alone.

The ideal pet
A cat is extremely adaptable and is equally happy whether living in a small apartment or in a large house.

BUILDING A GOOD RELATIONSHIP

Bonding *(left)*
Unlike a dog, a cat's affection and trust have to be earned, but once you have established a bond, it can last for life. The more you observe your cat's behavior, the better you will understand its basic nature and its likes and dislikes.

Early lessons *(below)*
A cat makes an excellent pet for a child old enough to appreciate how an animal should be picked up and handled *(see page 41)*. A child who is brought up in a household with pets will learn to appreciate the responsibilities of caring for another living creature.

Making friends *(above)*
Continue to play games with your cat from kittenhood through to adulthood *(see pages 42–43)*. Most cats will pounce on a length of string or chase a bouncy ball, and some can even be taught tricks.

WHY CHOOSE A CAT?

Cats versus dogs *(left)*
Cats are by nature more independent than dogs and are easier to keep. A dog needs to be taken for a walk on a leash at least twice a day, whereas a cat is quite capable of exercising and amusing itself, although it does enjoy human company.

Dogs are more demanding pets than cats

The appeal of cats *(right)*
Stroking a cat can help relieve stress, and the feel of a purring cat on your lap conveys a strong sense of security and comfort. Do not expect your cat to be sociable on demand – it will appreciate some privacy and peace and quiet.

Cats versus other small pets *(left)*
Cats are much easier to keep clean than other pets, such as birds and rodents, whose cages must be cleaned daily. Other animals make less rewarding pets because they are not as responsive and lead shorter lives.

CAT OWNERSHIP WORLDWIDE
In Great Britain and North America, there are now almost as many cats as dogs. Over 30 percent of households in North America and 24 percent in Europe own a cat.

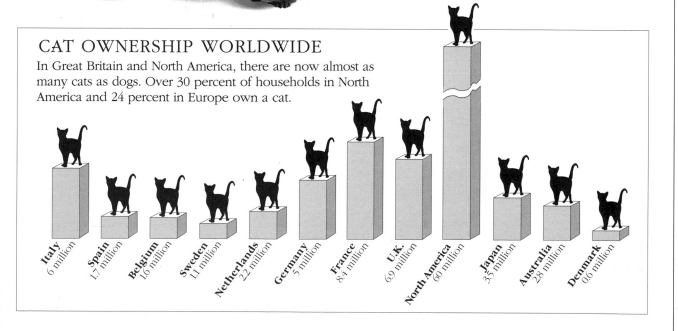

Italy	Spain	Belgium	Sweden	Netherlands	Germany	France	U.K.	North America	Japan	Australia	Denmark
6 million	1.7 million	1.6 million	1.1 million	2.2 million	5 million	8.4 million	6.9 million	60 million	3.5 million	2.8 million	0.6 million

BASIC CAT TYPES

There are over a hundred recognized breeds of domestic cat. The main feline features that vary are body type, eye color, coat color, and length of coat. Although some pedigree cats are natural breeds, many others are the result of careful breeding. Most cats are of no particular breed and are crosses of different types. These are what we have come to know as "housecats." They can have long or short hair and come in a variety of different colors, the most common of which are tabby, tortoiseshell, ginger, and black.

BODY TYPES

Cobby cat
Pedigree Longhair breeds have stocky, rounded bodies with sturdy, short legs and round faces. Their body type is described as cobby. Other characteristics of this longhaired cat include a broad head and round eyes.

Muscular cat
Most shorthaired cats have muscular builds with sturdy, short legs. This is the most common of the different feline body shapes. Some pedigree cats, such as British and Exotic Shorthairs, have more compact bodies.

Foreign longhaired cat
There are a few breeds of longhaired cat that have slim bodies that differ from the usual cobby type. This group includes Asian breeds such as the Balinese, Angora, and Somali. They have long bodies, with slim legs, wedge-shaped heads, and almond-shaped eyes.

The coat is less woolly and full than that of Pedigree Longhairs

Exotic shorthaired cat

An exotic or oriental cat has an elegant, slim body that is very different from the muscular build of other shorthaired cats. This type of cat has long, slender legs, a wedge-shaped head, large, pointed ears, and slanting eyes. Breeds such as the Siamese, Abyssinian, Tonkinese, and Egyptian Mau all have this slim build.

The coat is very fine and short

TYPES OF EYES

Cats' eyes come in three basic shapes: round, slanted, and almond-shaped. Their colors are basically green, yellow to gold and, most rarely, blue. However, there is a wide range of different shades within these three basic colors. Most non-pedigree cats have green eyes.

British Smoke Shorthair

Non-pedigree Tabby

White Pedigree Longhair

British Tortoiseshell-and-White

Maine Coon

Birman

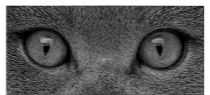
British Blue Shorthair

Egyptian Mau

Snowshoe

British Tortoiseshell Shorthair

Burmilla

Balinese

Chapter 2

BASIC CARE

W E WANT our cats to live long and happy lives – they contribute so much to our own. A cat is not a demanding pet to keep; all it needs is adequate feeding, regular grooming, and proper veterinary care. A cat thrives best with a sympathetic owner who can devote a lot of attention to it and join in with games. You can keep your cat healthy by ensuring that it is protected from diseases by yearly vaccination and that it is neutered to prevent unwanted kittens. Given time and tender loving care, you will build up trust with your cat. However, it may always regard some aspects of feline care, such as traveling in its carrier and visits to the vet, as tiresome.

BECOMING A CAT OWNER

Bringing a cat into your home will change your life. The benefits of having a feline companion bring with them obligations and, unless you are prepared to make sure that your pet will receive the care and attention that it needs, cat owning is not for you. Having decided that you want to share your home with a cat, you need to decide what type of feline is best for you. Do you want a kitten or an adult cat? A pedigree or a non-pedigree? A longhaired or a shorthaired cat?

THE CAT FOR YOUR LIFESTYLE

Purebred cats
The temperament of a well-bred cat can be fairly reliable. Choose a breed with characteristics that you think fit in with your lifestyle.

Non-pedigree cats *(left)*
A cat may not come with papers, but it can still make a wonderful companion. You can go to your local animal shelter and find one just right for you.

Kittens *(above)*
Kittens demand lots of attention and need to be house trained. They adapt to a new home better than adult cats, so a kitten is a good choice if you already have other pets.

One cat or two? *(right)*
If you are out during the day, consider living with two cats. They will amuse each other and will wreak less havoc in your home.

Mother and kittens *(above)*
Think carefully about the implications of not having your cat neutered *(see pages 154–155)*. There are not enough homes for the cats already born.

Longhaired cats *(above)*
The Ragdoll is an especially docile cat, set apart by its reputed tendency to relax all its muscles when picked up and cradled. Longhaired cats are generally sweet natured, gentle, and enjoy a quiet life.

Oriental cats *(left)*
Siamese, Burmese, and other oriental cats are very sociable. They are lively, inquisitive, and love people. They can also be very vocal – if you do not give them enough attention.

Show cats *(above)*
If you intend to show your cat it will require special attention and grooming. A first-class show cat represents a significant investment in terms of time and money.

WHERE TO OBTAIN A CAT

It is far better to obtain a cat from a friend, neighbor, animal shelter, or recommended cat breeder than from a pet shop. Never take an animal on impulse because you have fallen for its charm. Always examine a cat very carefully before taking it home.

Friends
Friends are a reliable source of kittens since you will probably know the mother.

Animal shelters
Animal shelters often have plenty of kittens and adult cats needing good homes.

Local vets
Your vet may know of cats needing a home. Check the cat's health first.

Breeders
A breeder is a good source of purebred kittens. Specify whether you want a cat for showing.

ESSENTIAL EQUIPMENT

Before you bring a cat into your home, it is essential that you make preparations for the new arrival. A cat is not very expensive to keep, but it must be provided with a litter box, a scratching post, separate food and water bowls, a carrier, and a brush and comb. If you wish, you can also provide it with other useful items, such as a comfortable basket or bed, and a cat flap.

Brush
A brush is essential for longhaired cats. Buy the best quality bristle brush that you can afford.

Comb
A fine-toothed metal comb is useful for grooming a shorthaired cat, but a wide-toothed comb is better for a longhaired variety.

Food bowls
Every cat must have its own bowl and feeding utensils, which should always be kept clean.

Litter box and litter scoop
Even a kitten or adult cat that is allowed outside will need to be provided with a plastic litter box. This needs to be cleaned daily; a plastic scoop allows the used litter to be removed without soiling the hands.

Cat basket *(below)*
A basket should be comfortable, warm, and easy to clean.

Cat carrier *(right)*
There is a wide
range of different
carriers available
(see page 48).

Water bowls
Fresh water that is
replenished daily
should always be
available for a cat.

Cat bed *(right)*
Beds come in many
different varieties,
including beanbags
and hammocks.

CHOOSING A KITTEN

You can share your life with your cat for 14 years or more, so it is crucial that you choose a kitten that will grow up to be a well-adjusted, healthy adult. If you buy a kitten that is weak and sickly just because you feel sorry for it, or to ensure that it gets veterinary treatment, you may be letting yourself in for large medical fees and a lot of heartache. However, if you purchase a kitten and it falls ill or does not improve within a week or two, you may be able to take it back to the breeder, provided that you have both agreed upon such action before buying the kitten.

When choosing a kitten, you should take into consideration how it was reared and its mother's state of health. You should watch the kitten interact with both people and its littermates to determine its personality. Ideally, kittens should not be removed from the litter until they are ten to twelve weeks of age.

Nine-week-old kitten (actual size)
A healthy kitten has a firm, muscular body and feels much heavier than it looks when you pick it up.

The nose is velvety and slightly damp

The eyes are bright and clear

The mouth and gums are pink in color

The fur is soft and smooth to the touch

The limbs show no signs of lameness

The tail has no kink or other deformity

WHAT TO LOOK FOR WHEN CHOOSING A KITTEN

The ears should be clean with no discharge. Constant scratching may be a sign of mites.

The eyes should be clear, bright, and free from discharge. The third eyelid should not be showing.

The nose should be cool and damp, without any nasal discharge or crusting around the nostrils.

The mouth and gums should be pale pink in color and the breath odor-free.

The abdomen should be slightly rounded but not potbellied, which may be a sign of roundworms.

The coat is a good pointer to how healthy the kitten is; it should be glossy with no signs of fleas.

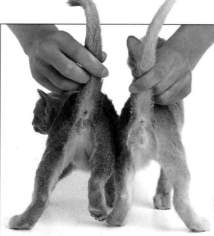

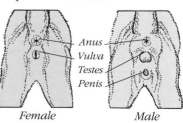

The rear should be clean, with no signs of diarrhea or any discharge from the genitals.

SEXING A KITTEN
The female kitten's anus and vulva are very close together; the anus and penis are farther apart in the male.

Anus
Vulva
Testes
Penis

Female   *Male*

FIRST INTRODUCTIONS

If you already have pets, introducing a new cat into your household has to be managed carefully. An adult cat, in particular, will react strongly to the presence of another feline and may defend its territory. The resident pets have to be slowly accustomed to the newcomer, and this will take time and a lot of patience. Feed the animals separately and supervise all meetings for the first few weeks.

ADDING A CAT TO YOUR HOME

A kitten pen
In the security of a pen, two kittens get used to their new home.

INTRODUCING A CAT TO A DOG

Do not let the dog get too close

1 Use a leash to control the dog so that it does not bark or chase and scare the cat. Wait until the dog and cat have become accustomed to each other before allowing the dog off the leash.

2 After a couple of weeks of careful supervision, the cat and dog should have accepted each other's presence and should be able to sit in the same room. Eventually, the cat may become bold enough to actually play with the dog!

INTRODUCING A KITTEN TO AN ADULT CAT

1 Allow the cat to investigate the carrier in which the kitten arrived. If the reaction is neutral, proceed with introducing the kitten. Separate them if the cat attacks the kitten.

The cat will be wary of the kitten at first

2 It may take up to a month for the cats to settle down. It is usually easier to bring a young kitten, rather than an adult cat, into a house that already has another feline.

INTRODUCING A KITTEN TO SMALL PETS

Rabbits
A kitten can frighten a rabbit by clambering all over it. An adult cat should not be left unsupervised with a pet rabbit.

Guinea pigs
A guinea pig will be a source of fascination to a kitten. Never let rodents out of their cages when an adult cat is on the prowl.

Happy pets
Provided all your pets have their own separate living areas, peaceful coexistence between different species can be achieved.

BASIC ROUTINES

You cannot train a cat in the same way as a dog to obey specific commands, but it does need to be house trained in order to live in a human household. Because a cat is by nature a remarkably clean and fastidious animal, it usually learns very quickly how to use a litter box. A cat is a fairly undemanding companion. All it really needs is regular feeding, grooming, clean toilet facilities, routine health care, and a corner for its bed or basket where it can enjoy a quiet catnap. However, it is important to maintain a daily routine in caring for your cat, since it will be unhappy if it is ignored or if its feeding schedule is erratic. Plan well ahead before introducing a cat into your home. It will be easier for your pet to adjust to its surroundings if essential items *(see pages 28–29)*, such as a litter box, food bowl, and basket, are installed before it arrives in the home.

LITTER TRAINING

House training
Cats are quick to learn how to use a litter box. Keep the box in a place readily accessible to the cat, but with some degree of privacy.

TYPES OF LITTER BOX

Covered box
A timid cat will appreciate the privacy of an enclosed litter box.

Ordinary box
Place the box in a quiet corner.

TYPES OF LITTER

Reusable Washable, non-absorbent litter.

Fuller's earth Based on natural clay.

Lightweight Very convenient to carry.

Wood-based Good for absorbing liquid waste.

ESTABLISHING ROUTINES

Playtime

Play is vital for a cat's physical and emotional development. Try to spend 10 to 15 minutes twice a day, playing with your cat. Continue the games into your cat's adulthood to maintain a good relationship with your pet *(see pages 42–43)*.

Feeding time

Nourishing meals must be provided for your cat. Prepared foods from reliable manufacturers are the safest and most convenient option. They can be supplemented with the occasional fresh food treat.

Bedtime

Every cat should have a quiet spot for its bed. Cats can sleep for up to 16 hours a day. Do not let your cat stay outside at night, since this is an especially dangerous time.

Regular grooming

Whether your cat is longhaired or shorthaired, it needs to be groomed regularly. Grooming should be started as young as possible *(see page 67)*.

TRAINING A CAT

A cat will not do anything that it does not want to, so training has to concentrate on gently enticing your pet to modify its natural behavior. You must keep in mind that a cat is not behaving badly when it scratches a favorite chair – it is keeping its claws trim by stripping away their outer layers, as well as marking its territory with scent. If you want to protect your furniture, provide your cat with a scratching post. The younger your cat is the easier it will be to train it to use a post. If you have an enclosed, protected area, give your cat the freedom to come and go by installing a cat flap.

USING A SCRATCHING POST

Perch from which the cat can survey its surroundings

The rope is impregnated with catnip

Toy balls make the post more interesting

HOME-MADE POSTS

A log complete with bark makes an ideal, natural scratching post. A post can easily be made by attaching a piece of carpet to a wooden plank, pile-side down. Carpet pile does not provide enough "snag."

Training

Whenever your cat looks as if it is going to claw the furniture, caution it and lure it to the scratching post. The post can be made more attractive by rubbing a little catnip on it. Manufactured posts come in a range of designs; this one has a perch for the cat to sit on and balls with which it can play.

USING A CAT FLAP

The clear plastic door allows the cat to see outside

1 The cat flap should be positioned at the right height for the cat to step through, about 6 in (15 cm) from the base of the door. Begin training the cat to use the flap by propping it partly open, and then tempting the cat through with a little food on the other side.

The locking device keeps unwanted visitors out

The magnet worn on the cat's collar opens the flap

2 The cat will quickly learn to push open the door itself when it wants to go outside. An electromagnetic cat flap is useful for preventing strange cats from entering the house. This type of door can only be activated by a magnet. The latter should be worn on an elasticized collar.

6 in (15 cm)

TYPES OF CAT FLAP

Most cat flaps swing in two directions and have a magnetic strip along the sides to keep out drafts. Whatever the type of flap, it should be easy to open, so that the cat can push it with its head without the risk of getting its neck or paws stuck.

Standard cat flap
A standard cat flap like this one is inexpensive and easy to install but does not have a locking device.

Lockable cat flap
A locking device is useful if you want to prevent your cat from going outdoors at night and for keeping other cats out.

COLLARS AND LEADS

A cat does not need much in the way of accessories, but a collar with a nametag is essential, just in case your pet goes outside. A cat should be trained to wear a collar from an early age. Start by putting the collar on for a short period each day until the cat is used to wearing it. A collar with an identification tag giving the cat's name and your address and telephone number is useful in case of accidents and will help prevent your cat from being mistaken for a stray should it wander or get lost. If you take it for a walk outside, you will want to train it to walk in a harness and lead. This will take a lot of gentle coaxing, and even then you may not get your cat to go where you want. Cats that lack confidence should be left at home.

A collar must fit properly

Elasticized collar
A collar must have an elasticized section so that a cat can slip out of it should it get caught.

TYPES OF COLLAR AND LEAD

Flea collars are not suitable for young kittens and must be used as directed

Collars
There is a wide range of different collar designs. Always take the collar off when grooming to check for skin irritations.

There is a collar to suit every budget, ranging from the simple type to diamond-studded ones

A tartan collar is ideal for a fashion-conscious cat that needs a different collar for every day of the week

A harness is essential when training because a cat can slip out of a collar

A collar should have an elasticized safety section and felt backing and should be easily adjustable

You can cut down a collar intended for an adult cat to fit a kitten

Select a light leather or cord lead that is suitable for a cat

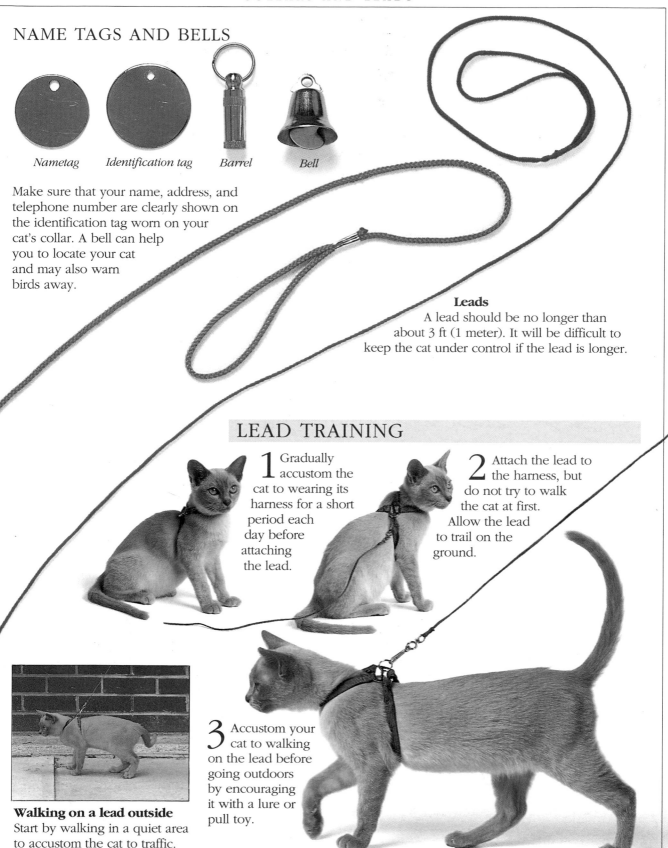

NAME TAGS AND BELLS

Nametag *Identification tag* *Barrel* *Bell*

Make sure that your name, address, and telephone number are clearly shown on the identification tag worn on your cat's collar. A bell can help you to locate your cat and may also warn birds away.

Leads
A lead should be no longer than about 3 ft (1 meter). It will be difficult to keep the cat under control if the lead is longer.

LEAD TRAINING

1 Gradually accustom the cat to wearing its harness for a short period each day before attaching the lead.

2 Attach the lead to the harness, but do not try to walk the cat at first. Allow the lead to trail on the ground.

3 Accustom your cat to walking on the lead before going outdoors by encouraging it with a lure or pull toy.

Walking on a lead outside
Start by walking in a quiet area to accustom the cat to traffic.

HANDLING A CAT

Physical contact is very important for establishing a close relationship with your pet. When holding or carrying a cat, you should allow it to adopt the position in which it feels most comfortable and talk to it in a reassuring way. A cat will soon let you know when it has had enough and wants to be left alone; a determined, protesting cat can be quite a handful. You should also learn where your cat likes to be stroked and which areas of its body are particularly sensitive. When handling a cat, take it in its own time and never use force or sudden movements, which will frighten it.

PICKING UP A CAT

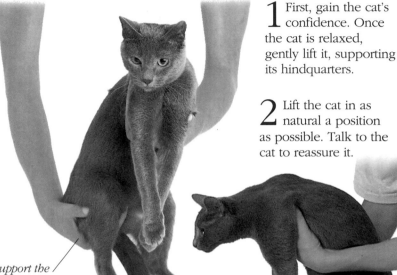

1 First, gain the cat's confidence. Once the cat is relaxed, gently lift it, supporting its hindquarters.

2 Lift the cat in as natural a position as possible. Talk to the cat to reassure it.

Support the rear and hind legs

3 Use one arm to support the cat's hindquarters, and the other for support and for gentle stroking.

Holding a cat
Cats enjoy being held for brief periods, but they do like to be in control of their own movements and will usually only feel at ease in the arms of a human whom they know and trust. Some individuals can be trained to sit on their owners' shoulders.

CHILDREN AND CATS

Best of friends
Some cats can be frightened by children, who need to be taught how to stroke and play with their pet. This cat has complete confidence in its young companion.

Holding a kitten
Children find kittens irresistible and should be discouraged from picking them up and cuddling them.

First introductions
Introduce a cat to a child very gradually; initial contact should be confined to gentle stroking.

Correct handling
Physical contact should not be forced or prolonged if a cat wants to be put down.

Do not try to hold on to a struggling cat

STROKING ZONES

Chest and ears
Most cats enjoy being stroked or rubbed around the ears and chest.

Neck and back
A relaxed cat appreciates being stroked on its neck and back.

Abdomen
Do not stroke a cat's abdomen and back legs unless you know it well.

PLAYING WITH A CAT

One of the many joys of owning a cat is watching it play. Learning to play is essential for the development of kittens because it teaches them important skills that they will need as adults. After the age of about six months, a cat loses some of its playfulness. It prefers to save its energies for the more serious business of hunting and may need to be encouraged to play games.

You can make any game more appealing for your cat by joining in, but the best way to keep a cat playful is to provide it with a companion. A couple of cats brought up in the same household will continue to play together in adulthood.

Catnip mice

Small balls

Fluffy feather

Feather and string

Toys
Some favorite toys include catnip mice, sacks filled with dried catnip, bouncy balls, and feathers.

Catnip sack

SOLITARY GAMES

Ping-pong ball
A small, bouncy ball is an ideal toy for your cat to pat and push around with its paws. Be prepared to retrieve it from behind doors and underneath armchairs.

Catnip mouse
If your cat likes catnip, this toy will have it purring in ecstasy. Catnip toys do lose their scent after a while and need to be replaced.

Cat's cradle (left)
A ball of yarn makes an irresistible toy. A cat will enjoy trailing it around chairs and table legs. Never allow your cat to play with thread or yarn unsupervised, since it may swallow it.

GAMES FOR SHARING

Hide-and-seek
A cardboard box is ideal for playing games of hide-and-seek. After sniffing every corner of a box, a cat likes to hide itself away, but once inside it will probably be ambushed by its feline companion.

Mouse on a string *(above)*
A cat is fascinated by any object that is dangled or pulled in front of its nose. A piece of string tied to a short pole will keep your cat amused.

A cat tries to paw a feather held just out of its reach

Fun with feathers
A feather is a good toy for tickling and playing with your cat, but watch out for its claws. If you do not move your hand away very quickly, you are likely to get scratched.

Feline fishing *(above)*
Trail a feather on a piece of string or cord for your cat to chase. Drag the feather slowly in front of the cat's paws and wait for it to pounce, then slowly reel it in.

Pouncing practice
A cat will be fascinated by a cardboard tube and will wait hopefully for something interesting to emerge. Reward its patience by giving it a catnip toy to play with or a tasty cat treat.

THE OUTDOOR CAT

Where it is possible, a cat will enjoy being allowed outside, and will set up its own territory to patrol and defend, even if this consists of only a small yard. A cat marks its home ground with scent by scratching trees and rubbing itself against fence posts. Urine spraying also acts as a warning to other cats to keep away, especially when it is carried out by tomcats. All these feline signals have to be reinforced regularly, since they act as markers to other cats. The more recent the scent, the more other cats take notice. To prevent unwanted pregnancies, never allow an unaltered cat outside.

Climbers
While all cats enjoy climbing for exercise or to survey their territory, kittens can sometimes become frightened by the height and must be helped down. On the whole, however, mature cats have no difficulty in retracing their steps to the ground when they are ready to do so.

Vantage point (left)
A roof, fence, or wall makes a good vantage point from which a cat can watch over its territory and make sure that no intruders trespass on its ground. From such a high point, the cat can also see the best hunting and resting places. All cats have favorite areas for sleeping or just watching.

An erect tail signifies alertness to everything that is going on

Cat patrol
A cat will need to patrol its territory regularly to defend it against other cats that might want to muscle in. It will also have to sniff out the scent of its rivals, so that it does not get into trouble by straying into another feline's territory.

The cat's sensitive nose investigates every scent

COMMON DANGERS IN THE YARD

Practically every yard has some hazards in it, since a large number of plants are toxic to animals *(see page 167)*. Even though a cat will not normally eat garden plants, it is wise to keep poisonous ones to a minimum when laying out your garden. A high fence, preferably with the top sloping inward, may be needed if there is a busy road nearby, both to keep your pet in and to keep out other cats.

All poisonous materials should be kept out of a yard where there are cats or securely locked away. Substances that are toxic to cats include slug pellets (especially metaldehyde), antifreeze, creosote and other wood preservatives, insecticides, and herbicides. If a cat can get into a garage or garden shed, it may also be at risk from paint, oil, gasoline, sharp tools, and carbon monoxide fumes.

Dangers in the yard

Poisonous plants, garden chemicals, dogs, and rival cats are among the common hazards for a cat in even the most innocent-looking yard. A kitten may fall into a pond or swimming pool and be unable to get out.

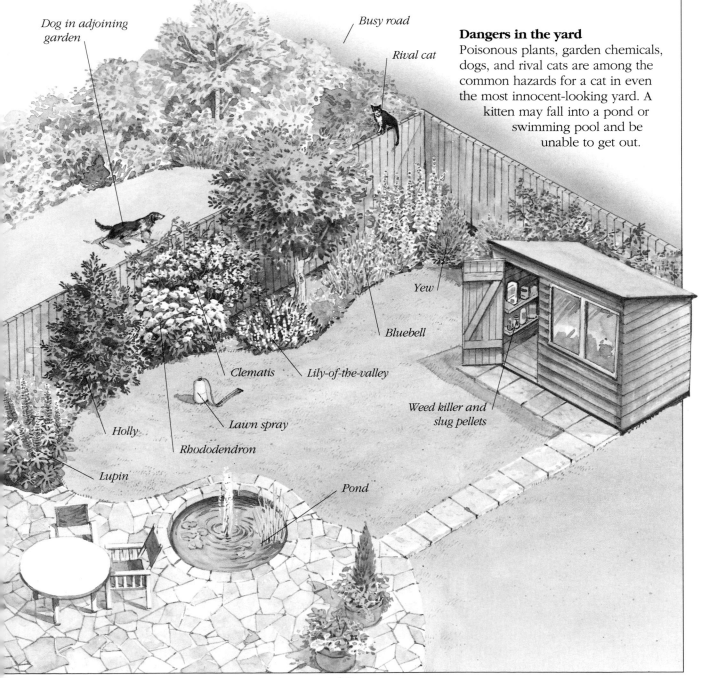

Dog in adjoining garden

Busy road

Rival cat

Yew

Bluebell

Clematis

Lily-of-the-valley

Holly

Lawn spray

Rhododendron

Lupin

Weed killer and slug pellets

Pond

THE INDOOR CAT

A cat is by its nature a very independent creature that likes to be able to come and go as it pleases. However, some cat owners living in large cities or high-rise apartments may find it impossible to let their pet outside and prefer to keep it safely confined to the home. Most cats can live quite happily indoors, as long as all their needs for amusement, exercise, and safety are provided. It is best to accustom a cat to being inside when it is still a kitten. Its litter box must be cleaned daily, and it should be provided with plenty of toys and games or, better still, a feline companion. You may want to try training your cat to walk on a lead for short trips outside the home *(see page 39).*

Best friends
A feline companion will ensure that an indoor cat never becomes bored when it is left alone.

OUTDOOR RUNS FOR CATS

Outdoor pens
If you wish to allow your cat access to the outside world while still keeping it safe, an outdoor run is the answer. It should be constructed of strong posts and wire netting and provided with a covered shelter in case of bad weather. A cat may also appreciate a tree or post for climbing and scratching.

INDOOR LAWN
Most cats enjoy chewing on grass, as a source of certain extra vitamins. If your cat is kept indoors, you should provide it with a pot of fresh greenery such as lawn grass, catnip, thyme, sage, chickweed or parsley.

Grass in pots
Sow some seeds in a pot for a regular supply of fresh grass.

COMMON DANGERS IN THE HOME

A home can be full of hazards for a cat, especially a kitten or a new arrival. Cats are naturally curious, so washing machines, tumble driers, refrigerators, and ovens should never be left open. Hot irons, tea kettles, and saucepans full of boiling liquids should not be left unattended. Kittens may chew electrical cord, and some cats may chew plants and cut flowers out of boredom. Some houseplants, such as ivies, philodendrons, and poinsettias, can be toxic (see page 167). Fragile ornaments can be knocked off shelves by exploring cats. Open fires should always be protected by a guard, even when unlit. Other dangers include detergents and chemicals, threaded needles, pins, and plastic bags. An open window on an upper floor can lead to a cat falling and injuring itself.

Indoor hazards

Any home can be full of potential dangers for a cat, especially a kitten or a newcomer. They range from open fires and poisonous houseplants to electrical equipment and cooking utensils.

Open window
Food left out
Boiling saucepan
Sharp knife
Electric coffee pot
Poisonous houseplant
Breakable ornaments
Trash bin
Washing machine door open
Hot iron
Household detergent
Plastic bags
Open fire
Pins and needles
Electrical cord

TRAVELING AND MOVING HOUSE

Cats do not adjust to travel as readily as dogs and should be confined to carriers for the duration of any trip. Before taking a cat anywhere, you should familiarize it with its carrier. Leave the carrier out and open, and put a treat inside to tempt the cat to investigate. It is essential that your cat sees the carrier in a positive light. A warm blanket will provide good insulation in cold weather, while in very hot weather you may need to cover the carrier with a damp cloth.

Never leave a cat unattended in a car on a hot day, even with a window open, since it may get overheated. Do not allow a cat to travel loose in a car. It may become agitated or get in the driver's way.

TRANSPORTING A CAT

Wire carrier
Well ventilated, secure, and easily cleaned, a plastic-coated wire carrier is ideal for moving a cat. Line it with a towel or newspapers in case of accidents.

TYPES OF CARRIER

Wicker carrier *(left)*
Traditional wicker carriers give a cat some privacy, while allowing it to see out. The disadvantages of this type of carrier are that it is difficult to keep clean and may not be entirely "catsafe."

Plastic carrier *(right)*
Like wire carriers, lightweight plastic carriers are easy to disinfect and clean. Larger carriers will accommodate two cats if they are used to traveling together.

Cardboard carrier
A cardboard carrier is only suitable for emergencies or when taking a calm cat on a short journey.

PUTTING A CAT INTO A CARRIER

1 First close all the doors and windows. Allow the cat to use its litter box before being put into the carrier. Pick up the cat in a firm but gentle way. The cat may start to struggle when it sees the carrier.

CAR SICKNESS

A cat that is a very bad traveler may be tranquilized when being taken on a long journey. Consult your vet about obtaining and administering tranquilizers.

2 Lift the cat into the carrier, supporting its hind legs. The carrier should always be lined with newspapers or a towel, even if you are only going on a short trip.

The carrier should be lined in case of accidents

Make sure the carrier is fastened

3 Keep your grip on the cat until just before you secure the door. Given the chance, a cat will jump out and will become agitated if you have to chase it around the house.

MOVING

Confine your cat to a quiet room of the house while the furniture is being moved, so that it is not scared by all the commotion, or it may try to run away. Do not feed the cat before the journey, since this may make it sick if it does not travel well. When the furniture van has gone, put the cat in its carrier and take it to your new home. Upon arrival, allow the cat time to settle down and become accustomed to its surroundings. Provide it with food, water, and a litter box. Supervise its explorations of your new home for the first few days, watching for situations that may be hazardous for your cat.

Car travel
A cat must be confined for car travel.

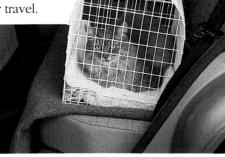

TRAVELING ABROAD AND CATTERIES

Vacations and travel abroad require careful planning by the cat owner. For all travel, whether by air, road, rail, or sea, a cat will have to be in a container approved by the carrying company and the U.S. government. For long journeys it will need food, water, and access to a litter box.

Although it is not advisable to sedate a cat for traveling, a vet can prescribe a tranquilizer if you have a nervous animal. A pregnant or nursing queen and young kittens should not be taken on long journeys.

If you cannot take your cat with you, make sure that it will be cared for properly in your absence, whether by friends, neighbors, at a cattery, or by a "cat-sitting" agency.

AIR TRAVEL

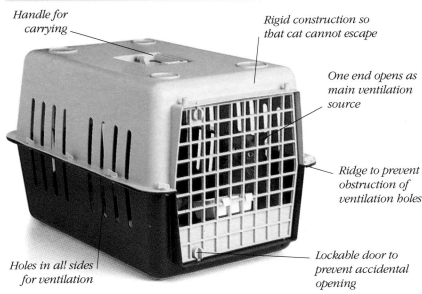

Handle for carrying

Rigid construction so that cat cannot escape

One end opens as main ventilation source

Ridge to prevent obstruction of ventilation holes

Holes in all sides for ventilation

Lockable door to prevent accidental opening

Feline freight
Cats being transported by air must be contained in a carrier like the one above. Such a container must be strong and light, and allow plenty of ventilation, especially for long journeys. Instructions for feeding and watering and the owner's name and address should be clearly marked.

QUARANTINE
In the United States, traveling between states with an animal is forbidden unless you have the required vaccination and health documents. You will need to check with each state you enter regarding the laws on vaccinations.

If you take your cat abroad, you will need to comply with the regulations issued by the transportation company and the country you are visiting. A vet can advise you on regulations and which authorities you need to contact. The penalties for smuggling cats are severe, since they represent a potential health risk to humans.

Confinement
A cat taken abroad may have to spend time in quarantine either upon arrival or on return to its home country to prevent the spread of rabies.

BOARDING YOUR CAT

You should select a cattery well in advance of your vacation. Inspect the premises and make all the arrangements in good time, since many establishments are booked for months ahead. The cattery should be spotlessly clean and tidy, and the cats well cared for. The cats should be able to look out and see each other, but should be kept apart to prevent the spread of infection. All feeding and drinking bowls must be kept clean and sterile, and cat beds should be disposable, or of a material that can be thoroughly disinfected for each new occupant. You should inform the staff if your cat has special dietary needs, and you must ensure that your pet's vaccinations are up-to-date. The cattery should allow you to leave your cat several items to remind it of home, such as a favorite toy. There must be effective security at the cattery, with at least two barriers to the outside world to prevent the escape of boarders or the entrance of strange cats.

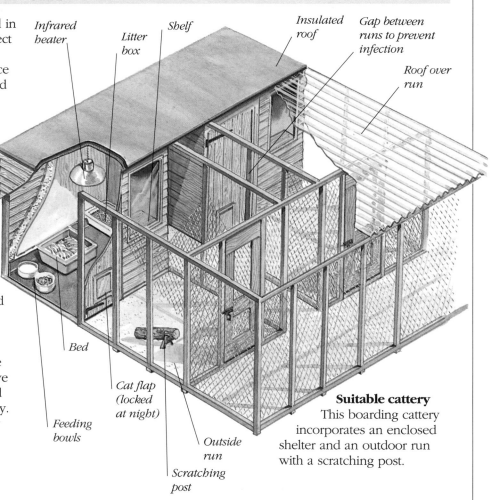

Infrared heater

Litter box

Shelf

Insulated roof

Gap between runs to prevent infection

Roof over run

Bed

Feeding bowls

Cat flap (locked at night)

Scratching post

Outside run

Suitable cattery
This boarding cattery incorporates an enclosed shelter and an outdoor run with a scratching post.

Communal cattery
Some boarding catteries have larger chalets for a nursing queen and her kittens, or for several adult cats from one household. Cats from different households should not share the same accommodation, and, in some areas, this is illegal. Many catteries have longterm facilities for cats that have to be boarded for long periods. Fees vary according to the facilities provided and are usually payable when a cat is picked up.

KEEPING A CAT HEALTHY

One of the responsibilities of caring for your cat involves taking it to the vet for regular checkups, vaccinations, and boosters. This essential part of feline maintenance should start from the first day that you bring your kitten home and continue through to its old age. You should choose a vet in your area who specializes in treating small animals. If the cost of veterinary care is a problem, you may be able to find a low-cost animal clinic in your neighborhood.

CHOOSING A VET

How to find a vet
Ask cat-owning friends to recommend a veterinary practice in your area. Find out what services are available, the fees charged, the consulting hours, and what the arrangements are in the event of an emergency.

You and your vet
A vet will advise you on keeping your cat healthy.

USING A VET

You should register your new cat with a vet as soon as you bring it home, and arrange for it to have a complete medical checkup to make sure that it is healthy. If you suspect that your pet is sick, it is advisable to take it to a vet as soon as possible. Never try to treat your cat at home without first obtaining veterinary advice. It will usually be impossible for you to make a correct diagnosis yourself, and your cat's condition is likely to worsen if you delay seeking professional treatment.

HEALTH INSURANCE

You may wish to take out a health insurance policy in case your cat falls ill. In return for paying a yearly premium, the pet insurance will cover most of the vet's fees for any course of treatment. It will not cover routine treatments such as vaccinations or neutering operations. Many pet insurance companies will also pay out a lump sum if a cat is killed in an accident, lost, or stolen.

BASIC HEALTH CARE

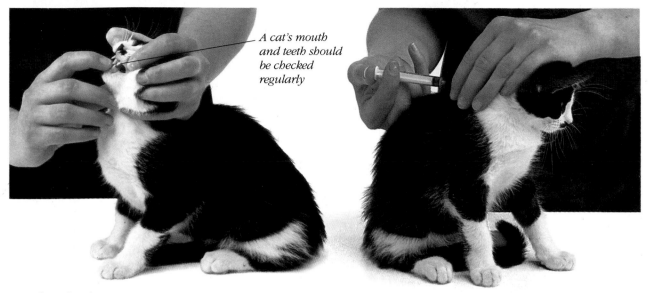

A cat's mouth and teeth should be checked regularly

Regular checkups
Keep a watch on your kitten's health by looking out for unusual behavior and by taking it for regular checkups.

Protection from diseases
A kitten must be vaccinated to protect it against infections such as Feline Infectious Enteritis.

HEALTH CHECKLIST
When you contact your local vet, it is helpful to be able to supply some details of its history. This is a list of questions that you may be asked about your cat:
- Is it alert and active?
- Is it eating and drinking?
- Is it vomiting or retching?
- Is it passing urine and feces normally?
- Is it coughing or sneezing?
- Is it pawing at its eyes or ears?
- Is it showing any signs of pain?

Vaccinations
A kitten should be vaccinated at about eight or nine weeks of age.

TRACING A CAT
If your cat is missing, start by searching your home and yard, since it may simply be locked in a cupboard. Once you have looked in all the obvious places, ask your neighbors for help. Put notices with a description and photograph of your cat in local shop windows, and offer a reward for its return.

You can contact the animal welfare organizations in your area to find out if your pet has been picked up, and local vets in case it has been involved in an accident. Do not give up hope. Cats have a great ability to survive, and there are cases of pets returning home after periods of several months.

A cat that goes outside must wear a collar and an identification disc engraved with your name and telephone number. Alternatively, a tiny identity microchip can be implanted under the skin of the neck. Consult your vet for advice.

Chapter 3
FEEDING

FELINE NUTRITION is an exacting science, since cats are carnivores with very special nutritional requirements. All cats require regular meals of wholesome, high-protein food and a constant supply of fresh water. Cats are by their nature very careful eaters, preferring their food to be fresh and served in a clean bowl. They will turn their noses up at stale food or at any that is served directly from the refrigerator. The nutritional state of a healthy cat is reflected in its appearance; it will have a shiny coat, bright eyes, an alert demeanor, and supple muscle tone. A good-looking, healthy cat is your reward for feeding your pet a well-balanced diet.

CORRECT FEEDING

A cat's unique nutritional needs make it a very demanding animal to feed *(see pages 58–59)*. It is also a very careful eater that quickly rejects its food if it does not have the right smell or if it is served at the wrong temperature. Its keen senses of smell and taste allow it to detect whether food is less than fresh. Try to make sure that your cat is fed at the same time each day and always in the same place.

Sometimes a cat supplements its diet by catching and eating small prey animals, but this does not mean that it is hungry or that you can prevent it from hunting by feeding it more. A cat hunts through instinct, and even a well-fed pet may catch mice given the opportunity.

Protein is essential for the growth and repair of tissues and for the regulation of metabolic processes

Essential fatty acids help give a sheen to a cat's coat

Vitamin A is essential for healthy eyes

Calcium and vitamin D are needed to build healthy bones and teeth

Carbohydrates add fiber to a cat's diet and provide additional energy

Optimum health
A well-fed cat is active and alert; its eyes are bright and its coat is glossy.

FEEDING EQUIPMENT

Even if you have more than one cat, each animal should have its own food and water bowls. You will also need to set aside a can opener, fork, spoon, and knife specially for serving your cat's food. All equipment must be washed after each meal. You can store your pet's utensils in a plastic box so that they do not get mixed up with the household supply. Plastic lids are useful for resealing opened cans. An automatic feeder has a timing device that allows it to open at preset times. It is only suitable if you are leaving your cat for no longer than 24 hours.

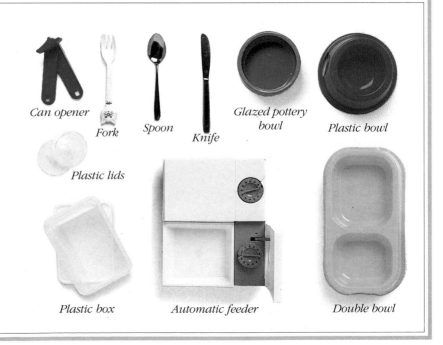

Can opener

Fork

Spoon

Knife

Glazed pottery bowl

Plastic bowl

Plastic lids

Plastic box

Automatic feeder

Double bowl

GUIDELINES FOR FEEDING

Ten basic rules

1 Feed prepared foods only from a reputable manufacturer.
2 Do not feed a cat food intended for a dog or other pets.
3 Always keep food bowls and feeding utensils clean.
4 Do not give a cat any food that is even slightly spoiled.
5 Carefully remove any small bones from fish and chicken.
6 Serve food at room temperature.
7 Dispose of uneaten food once the cat has walked away.
8 Keep a watch on your cat's weight, and do not let it overeat.
9 Do not put reheated food back in the refrigerator.
10 Consult a vet if your cat has refused food for 24 hours.

Do not give a cat too many scraps

Overfeeding
Feed your cat two to three small meals a day, following the manufacturer's recommendations. Do not give many snacks between meals.

Competition for food
A little competition makes for healthy appetites. You will not find a fussy eater in a household where there is more than one cat.

WATER AND MILK

A cat gets most of the moisture that it requires from its food, and many felines seem to drink little. However, you should make sure that fresh water is available at all times. If a cat is fed dry food it will need to increase its water intake because these foods contain very little moisture. Restrict the amount of dry food if your cat is a poor water drinker. Although milk contains a lot of valuable nutrients, it is not essential for a feline diet and may cause diarrhea. As an alternative to cow's milk, try giving one of the lactose-reduced brands available.

Some cats are unable to digest milk

Milk
Milk may cause stomach upset, so give no more than one to two tablespoons in a day.

A Cat's Dietary Needs

Cats require certain dietary components and animal-derived nutrients. They are not vegetarians and, although they can digest some vegetable matter, they are unable to live long on a completely meat-free diet. A cat does not have a strict dietary need for greenery, but you should make sure it has access to grass as a source of certain vitamins, which it cannot obtain in sufficient quantities in its food. A cat may vomit after eating grass, since this helps it to clean out its system and to get rid of unwanted matter, such as hairballs. You should make sure that any chemicals or fertilizer used on your lawn are non-toxic to animals.

Eating grass
Although a cat may sometimes chew grass, it cannot digest much vegetable matter.

YOUR CAT'S WEIGHT

An average adult cat should weigh about 9–11 lb (4–5 kg). Although cats do not vary in size as much as dogs, a cat's weight does vary according to the type of breed. A small cat may weigh only 5½ lb (2.5 kg), and a large cat as much as 12 lb (5.5 kg). The following is a list of average weights:

Feline obesity is usually due to a combination of overfeeding and lack of exercise. Neutered and elderly cats are most commonly affected. The occasional cat may have a hormonal problem, but a cat usually becomes fat because it is eating more food than it requires. A very overweight cat will have a large abdomen that hangs down. Its breathing is labored, and it soon becomes less active. Carrying the excess weight puts a strain on the cat's heart and makes it more susceptible to arthritis and other disorders in old age. If your cat is overweight, you should establish how much it is eating. It may be supplementing its diet by hunting, or it may be being fed elsewhere.

KITTENS

Age	Weight
One day	2½–5 oz (70–135 g)
One week	4–9 oz (110–250 g)
Three weeks	8–15 oz (215–420 g)
Four weeks	9–18 oz (250–500 g)
Five weeks	10–22 oz (290–620 g)
Six weeks	11–25 oz (315–700 g)
Seven weeks	14–31 oz (400–900 g)

ADULTS

Average	5½–12 lb (2.5–5.5 kg)
Pregnant	8–12 lb (3.5–5.5 kg)
Lactating	8–12 lb (3.5–5.5 kg)

REDUCING WEIGHT

Consult a vet to make sure that your cat's excess weight is not due to a medical problem. Cut down the cat's calorie intake by reducing the amount of food given under veterinary guidance. You can obtain a low-calorie diet from your vet or from a store that is especially formulated for feline weight loss.

Obesity
A very overweight cat has a shorter life expectancy than other cats.

THE NUTRITIONAL REQUIREMENTS OF AN ADULT CAT*

Component	Requirement	Source	Comments
Protein	A cat's diet should be made up of 28 percent protein. Kittens require much more.	Complete cat food, meat, fish, eggs, milk, and cheese.	Needs 20 percent more protein than a dog.
Fat	A cat's diet should be not less than 9 percent fat.	Animal and vegetable fats and oils.	Must have certain animal fats only found in meat and fish.
Carbohydrate	Should not be more than 40 percent of the cat's diet.	Cereals, rice, pasta, potatoes, and dry cat food.	A useful source of energy and extra fiber.
Calcium Phosphorus Sodium Potassium Magnesium Iron Copper Manganese Zinc Iodine	1 g per day 0.8 g per day 0.2 g per day 0.4 g per day 0.05 g per day 10 mg per day 0.5 mg per day 1.0 mg per day 4.0 mg per day 0.1 mg per day	All essential minerals are found in a healthy, balanced diet. Two of the most important dietary minerals, calcium and phosphorus, are found in animal products such as milk.	A cat is unlikely to suffer from a mineral deficiency if it is fed a balanced diet. An excess of minerals can be dangerous.
Vitamin A Vitamin B_1 (Thiamin) Vitamin B_2 (Riboflavin) Vitamin B_6 Pantothenic acid Niacin Folic acid Vitamin B_{12} Choline Taurine Vitamin C Vitamin D Vitamin E Vitamin K	550 international units per day 0.5 mg per day 0.5 mg per day 0.4 mg per day 1.0 mg per day 4.5 mg per day 0.1 mg per day 0.02 mg per day 200 mg per day 100 mg per day No dietary requirement 100 international units per day 8.0 mg per day No dietary requirement	All essential vitamins are found in a healthy, balanced diet. Vitamin A is found in liver, egg yolk, and butter. Vitamin B_1 is found in eggs, liver, cereals, and milk. Vitamin C is not needed in a cat's diet, since it can be manufactured in the body. Fish liver oils and animal fats are good sources of vitamin D.	Vitamins are essential for regulating all bodily processes. Any deficiency or excess may cause disease. Vitamin A poisoning is usually caused by ingestion of too much liver. A diet based on oily fish, such as tuna, can cause a deficiency of vitamin E.
Water	50–70 ml per kg of the cat's body weight.	Water is supplied in a balanced diet.	Water must always be available.

* Source: NRC National Academy of Sciences (1986), Washington, DC.

VITAMIN AND MINERAL SUPPLEMENTS

A variety of vitamins and minerals is essential to your cat's health and to the maintenance of its bodily functions. If you feed your cat a well-balanced, varied diet, extra vitamins should not be necessary since it will get all the nutrients it requires from its food. Giving vitamin and mineral supplements can be potentially harmful. An excess of vitamins A, D, or E, or of calcium and phosphorus, can cause serious health disorders, while an excess of cod liver oil can cause bone disease. Always seek the advice of a vet before giving supplements – they may be helpful if a cat has some metabolic problem, or for a pregnant queen or young kittens that require extra vitamins for growth.

Yeast tablets are a source of B vitamins.

Vitamin powder for adding to food.

Cat sweets containing added vitamins.

PREPARED CAT FOODS

Cats are nutritionally very demanding animals, requiring a high level of protein and fat. It is unwise to feed a cat on fresh foods alone and far safer to rely on a reputable manufacturer to supply a balanced diet. Most canned cat foods are complete: in other words, they contain all the necessary dietary constituents in the right proportion *(see page 59)*. Note the feeding recommendations given, and spend a little time reading the labels to check the nutritional content of the ingredients. Do not overfeed your cat, since it may become overweight and lazy.

TYPES OF CAT FOOD

Canned whitefish, flaked and with the bones removed

Canned foods
These contain meat, fish, gelling agents, fat, water, vitamins, and cereals.

Canned tuna chunks

Canned, medium-textured lamb chunks

Canned chicken and turkey with herbs

Salmon-flavored dry food

Chicken-flavored dry food

Beef-flavored dry food

Seafood-flavored dry food

Chicken-and-fish-flavored dry food

Dry foods
Usually fed as part of the diet. Fresh water must also always be available.

DAILY FEEDING REQUIREMENTS

Life stage	Type of complete food	Energy	Amount	Number of meals
Weaning to 8 weeks	*See page 153*	–	–	–
2–4 months	Canned kitten food	250–425 calories	10.50–18 oz (300–500 g)	3–4
4–5 months	Canned kitten food	425–500 calories	18–25 oz (500–700 g)	3–4
5–6 months	Canned kitten food	500–600 calories	25–28 oz (700–800 g)	2–3
6–12 months	Canned kitten food	600–700 calories	25–28 oz (700–800 g)	1–2
Adulthood*	Canned food	300–550 calories	13–28 oz (400–800 g)	1–2
	Semi-moist food	300–550 calories	13–26 oz (400–750 g)	1–2
	Dry snack food	Feed only as an occasional meal or mixed with a canned cat food.		–
Late pregnancy (last third)	Canned food	Feed at least a third more than normal, especially in the late stages of pregnancy *(see page 146)*.		2–4
Lactation	Canned food	Feed at least three times more than normal to satisfy the mother's and kittens' increased requirements.		2–4
Old age**	Canned food	Feed more where absorption is poor but less if the cat is inactive *(see page 139)*. Take veterinary advice.		1–2

*Cats vary in activity and may need less or more food overall. ** Cats with special dietary needs should be fed under veterinary supervision.

Semi-moist foods
Semi-moist foods can be alternated with canned or fresh foods.

Chicken-and-liver-flavored dry food

Beef-flavored semi-moist food

Liver-flavored semi-moist food

Chicken-flavored semi-moist food

Tuna-flavored dry food

Cat treats
Milk-flavored drops can be fed as a treat.

Liver-flavored dry food

Cat chews
Cat chews provide exercise for a cat's teeth and gums.

FRESH FOODS

The easiest way to ensure that your cat enjoys a balanced diet is to feed it a canned cat food produced by a reliable pet food manufacturer. However, you can feed your cat a meal of fresh food once or twice a week, to add variety and interest to its diet.

PREPARING FRESH FOODS

Fresh food treat
Your cat will like the taste and texture of fresh food and, if it is fed mainly on canned cat food, it will enjoy the change from its usual diet.

Cooked meat
Give your cat an occasional treat by cooking it some fresh beef, lamb, pork, or fish. Meat can be baked, grilled, or boiled and should be cooled and chopped into small chunks before serving.

Cooked meat with vegetables
Cooked carrots, peas, or greens can be added to meat for extra vitamins.

Cooked meat with pasta
Add a little cooked rice, pasta, or potato to your cat's food bowl to make the meat or fish go further. Vegetables and carbohydrates should only make up a very small proportion of your cat's diet.

Minced meat
Your cat will enjoy the occasional meal of cooked minced beef.

Cooked fish
White fish such as scrod, cod, or haddock is good for tempting a cat that is sick or that has a poor appetite. Fish should never be served raw; gently poach or steam it and remove bones.

Cooked poultry
Feed your cat all the leftover parts of a chicken, including the skin and giblets. Chop the chicken into small pieces, taking care to remove bones.

Canned sardines
Sardines, mackerel, or herring make a very nutritious treat.

Canned tuna
Canned tuna or salmon make a quick occasional meal. Bones should be removed before serving.

Scrambled egg
A lightly scrambled egg makes an excellent light meal. Never feed a cat raw egg whites.

Oatmeal
Oatmeal or baby cereal made with warm milk is appreciated by growing kittens. Do not add any sugar.

A satisfied cat
When a cat has finished eating a tasty meal, it will sit and wash its face with its paw.

Chapter 4

GROOMING

CATS ARE meticulous about keeping themselves clean and tidy. It is rare to see a healthy cat looking bedraggled. Cats only fail to groom themselves when they are sick or when they become elderly and frail. However, owners of longhaired cats do need to give their pets daily help with grooming. Fortunately, Pedigree Longhairs are generally placid  and good-natured and tend to enjoy the prolonged attention. If you accustom your cat to a grooming routine when it is young, it will be much easier when it gets older. A well-groomed cat, fed on a balanced diet, is a happy and active individual.

FIRST STEPS IN GROOMING

Grooming needs to be regular and frequent, but it does not have to take up much of your time unless you are preparing a cat for showing. If you accustom your pet to being groomed from a young age, it will be much easier to handle when it is an adult. Do not encourage a kitten to play with combs or brushes; if it continues to do this in later life, it is likely to scratch you and make grooming difficult.

Cats should have their claws trimmed regularly. If your cat is difficult, try doing just one or two claws a day. Declawing (the surgical removal of a cat's claws) deprives a cat of its natural means of defense, and may cause stress, resulting in behavioral problems. This practice is actively discouraged in most countries.

TRIMMING THE CLAWS

1 Light pressure on the cat's foot will expose the claws. A badly overgrown claw can grow into the paw pad and become infected, requiring veterinary treatment.

2 Using sharp clippers, cut off the white tip. Take care not to cut the sensitive quick.

GROOMING EQUIPMENT

Clippers   *Comb*   *Brush*   *Toothbrush*

You will need sharp nail or guillotine clippers for trimming your cat's claws, a bristle brush and comb for removing tangles in the coat, and a small, soft toothbrush for cleaning the teeth. All items should be used on only one cat.

WHERE TO TRIM THE CLAWS

It is safer to err on the cautious side and cut less claw rather than more. Cutting into the pink quick is painful and will result in bleeding. If you are unsure, ask a vet to show you how to trim your cat's claws correctly.

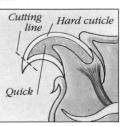

Cutting line
Hard cuticle
Quick

GROOMING A KITTEN

Use a comb to remove tangles

1 To calm the kitten and get it used to being groomed, stroke it gently before starting to use the brush and comb.

Hold the kitten still while gently stroking it

2 Comb through the kitten's coat from head to tail, looking for signs of fleas or other parasites at the same time *(see page 103)*.

3 Brush the fur to remove any dead hair. Pay particular attention to the legs and to the area between the toes, which can become soiled.

4 Gently brush the teeth and gums to accustom the kitten to a routine of dental hygiene from an early age *(see page 69)*.

Contented kitten
Grooming from kittenhood will strengthen the bond between you and your cat, and ensure that it develops into a pet that loves attention.

GROOMING A CAT'S FACE

Before grooming your cat, you should examine its eyes, ears, and teeth for signs of health problems and clean them if necessary. In most cases, the eyes and ears will only require a quick wipe with a cotton wad. Discoloration of the fur around the eyes may occur in Pedigree Longhair breeds as the result of blockage of the tear ducts and should be cleaned off. Consult a vet if the problem is recurrent. Your cat's teeth should ideally be brushed once a week.

The corners of the cat's eyes should be free from discharge

The ear flaps should be kept clean with no signs of dirt or dark wax

The teeth should be brushed weekly

Facial grooming
A cat's eyes, ears, and teeth need regular attention. Examine your cat once a week before grooming.

CLEANING THE EYES

1 A healthy cat's eyes rarely need much attention. Consult a vet if there is any sign of a discharge. Dampen a piece of cotton with water.

2 Wipe gently around each eye with a separate a cotton ball. Be careful not to touch the eyeball itself.

Remove staining from the corners of the eyes

3 Dry the fur around the eyes with a cotton ball or tissue. Owners of longhaired cats may need to remove any staining in the corners of the cat's eyes.

GROOMING EQUIPMENT

Cotton ball   Baby oil   Small bowl

Use a cotton ball dampened with warm water or baby oil.

CLEANING THE EARS

1 Inspect the cat's ears for signs of inflammation. Dark-colored wax may be caused by ear mites and requires veterinary attention *(see page 107).*

2 Moisten a cotton ball with a little baby oil and wipe away any dirt on the insides of the cat's ears.

3 Use a circular motion to gently clean the cat's ears but do not probe inside. Never poke cotton swabs in a cat's ears.

FELINE EARS

A cat's ear is a very delicate structure and should be treated with caution. Do not poke anything into the ear.

CLEANING THE TEETH

DENTAL EQUIPMENT

Toothbrush

Toothpaste   *Cotton swabs*

You need cotton swabs, a small toothbrush, and a tube of toothpaste.

Examine the gums and teeth

1 Gently open the cat's mouth to check that its gums and teeth are healthy. The gums should be firm and pink, and there should be no broken teeth.

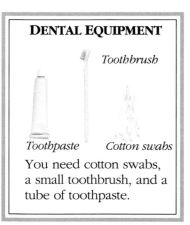

2 Accustom the cat to having its teeth brushed by lightly touching its gums with a cotton swab. Put a little pet toothpaste on the cat's lips so that it can get used to the taste.

3 After a couple of weeks, try brushing the cat's teeth using a small, soft toothbrush. Use either a pet toothpaste or salt and water.

COAT TYPES

Types of feline coat can be divided into the following basic categories: longhaired, shorthaired, curly, wirehaired, and hairless. A cat's coat has a topcoat of "guard" hairs that are thick and weatherproof. The undercoat consists of soft "down" hairs and bristly "awn" hairs. Different cat breeds have different grooming requirements.

Sphynx
The virtually hairless Sphynx has fine fur on its face, ears, paws, and tail. The skin should be regularly washed with a sponge.

COAT COLORS AND MARKINGS

The basic domestic cat has a tabby coat; all other coat markings are the result of selective breeding. There is an enormous variety of coat colors, including black, white, chocolate, blue, lilac, red, cream, and tortoiseshell. Coat patterns and shades also vary.

Red Tabby British Tabby Shorthair

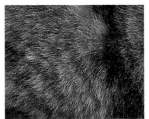

Silver Spotted British Spotted Shorthair

Tortoiseshell British Tortoiseshell Shorthair

Gray British Blue Shorthair

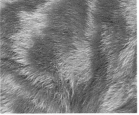

Gray and white British Bicolor Shorthair

Tortoiseshell British Tortoiseshell Shorthair

White Pedigree Longhair

Classic tabby Non-pedigree Shorthair

Chocolate tortoiseshell Cornish Rex

Pale gray Exotic Lilac Shorthair

Black British Black Shorthair

Brown Abyssinian

GROOMING DIFFERENT COAT TYPES

Shorthaired coat

A shorthaired cat requires little help with its appearance. However, grooming once a week will keep your cat's coat looking glossy and smooth.

Longhaired coat

Longhaired cats need the most attention and require daily grooming. Check for knotted fur on the abdomen and legs.

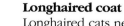

Angora (right)

An Angora's fur is fine and silky, with a tendency to wave. Grooming is particularly important in the spring, when this type of cat sheds its thick winter coat.

Rex (right)

A Rex's curly coat is very easy to groom. The fur is short, very silky to the touch, and particularly curly on the back and tail. Use a leather chamois to polish the coat.

Maine Coon

The fur of a Maine Coon is thick, but the undercoat is slight, which makes grooming easy. Gentle brushing every few days is all that is needed.

Exotic Shorthair

An Exotic Shorthair's coat is very dense and slightly longer than that of other shorthaired cats. This cat should be combed or brushed daily.

GROOMING A SHORTHAIRED CAT

Grooming your cat is a task that requires some patience, but your efforts will be rewarded if you make time for regular sessions. Cats are fastidious animals that wash themselves daily with immense care, but most appreciate and enjoy a little human help.

Start grooming your cat from as early an age as possible *(see page 67)*. An older cat that is set in its ways will not be so willing to submit itself to being brushed and handled. Establish a routine by setting aside a time for grooming, preferably when the cat is relaxed, perhaps after feeding. One or two sessions a week should be sufficient for most shorthaired cats.

As cats approach old age, or if they are ill, they become less competent and not so inclined to groom themselves properly, and may need more help in keeping neat and tidy.

GROOMING METHOD

1 With a metal comb, work through the cat's fur from head to tail to remove any dirt. Look for signs of fleas at the same time *(see page 103)*.

4 Every few weeks, apply a few drops of coat conditioner to help remove grease from the coat.

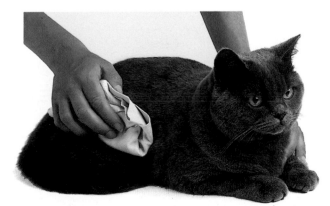

GROOMING EQUIPMENT

Metal comb *Bristle brush* *Rubber brush* *Leather chamois*

You will need a metal comb, bristle and rubber brushes, and a leather chamois. Keep all equipment as clean as possible.

5 Using a leather chamois or cloth, rub the conditioner into the coat to bring out the natural gleam.

2 Using a bristle brush, work along the lie of the coat. Brush all over the cat's body, including the chest and abdomen.

3 A rubber brush is excellent for removing dead hair and is particularly good for oriental-type cats with fine, short fur.

FLEAS AND PARASITES

While grooming your cat, examine its coat. You are unlikely to see many fleas, but you may be able to see flea droppings as black specks.

6 Stroking is enjoyable for your cat and will also help remove dead hair and keep the coat smooth.

British Blue
If your pet is fed a balanced diet and given plenty of daily care and attention, this will show in its glossy, healthy coat.

GROOMING A LONGHAIRED CAT

In the wild, a longhaired cat would only molt in the spring but, because domestic cats are kept in artificially lit and heated surroundings, they tend to molt throughout the year. Longhaired pedigree cats, in particular, need daily grooming sessions to keep their fur free from tangles. As well as keeping the coat clean, neat, and glossy, grooming serves to remove loose hairs and dead skin, and tones up the circulation and muscles.

It is important to accustom a longhaired kitten to being groomed from an early age *(see page 67)*. Neglect by an owner can have serious consequences, leading to a deterioration of the cat's coat, painful, matted hair, and even swallowed fur forming balls in the stomach.

If your cat dislikes being groomed, brush it very gently, a little at a time, until it becomes used to the process.

GROOMING METHOD

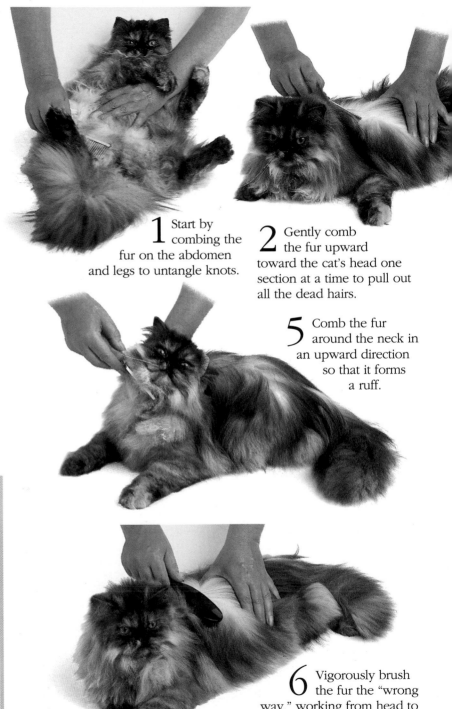

1 Start by combing the fur on the abdomen and legs to untangle knots.

2 Gently comb the fur upward toward the cat's head one section at a time to pull out all the dead hairs.

5 Comb the fur around the neck in an upward direction so that it forms a ruff.

6 Vigorously brush the fur the "wrong way," working from head to tail. Remove all talcum powder from the cat's coat before showing.

GROOMING EQUIPMENT

Wide-toothed comb *Talcum powder* *Bristle brush*

You will need a wide-toothed comb, talcum powder, and a natural bristle brush.

3 To help remove grease and dirt, sprinkle a little talcum powder onto the coat once a week.

4 To remove tangles, first sprinkle with talcum powder and then gently tease the knots out by hand.

MATTED FUR

Knots must be teased out by hand or with a mat-splitter, available at many pet supply stores. You may have to consult a vet for advice.

Do not forget to brush the cat's tail

7 Finally, make a parting down the middle of the tail and gently brush the fur out on either side.

Smoke Longhair
A longhaired cat's fur should be luxuriant and silky to the touch.

BATHING A CAT

Some people may be surprised at the idea of bathing a cat, but there may be times when this is essential, for instance if your cat's coat becomes contaminated with oil or grease. Show cats are bathed regularly, usually a few days before a show *(see page 182)*. Make sure you get everything ready beforehand, with the shampoo, towels, comb, brush, and pitcher for rinsing all within easy reach. You may need to enlist the aid of an assistant who can help you keep the cat calm and reassure it while it is being bathed.

Use a safe cat shampoo or a tearless shampoo, and be careful not to get any soap into the cat's eyes or ears. If you have a shorthaired cat, you may prefer to give it a dry shampoo. Rub warm bran into the coat, then vigorously brush it out.

BATHING METHOD

1 Fill a bath or large bowl with about 4 in (10 cm) of warm water. Test the temperature of the water and lift the cat firmly into the bath.

4 Rinse the cat, using plenty of warm water, until all traces of soap have been removed.

5 Lift the cat out of the bath and wrap it in a large, warm towel. Dry it off.

BATHING EQUIPMENT

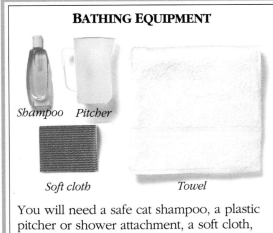

Shampoo   *Pitcher*

Soft cloth   *Towel*

You will need a safe cat shampoo, a plastic pitcher or shower attachment, a soft cloth, and a large towel for drying the cat off so that it does not catch a chill.

2 Wet the cat with a little shampoo mixed with warm water from the neck downward, using a pitcher or shower attachment.

3 Gently massage the shampoo well into the cat's coat. Take care not to get any soap into the cat's eyes or ears.

Do not put undiluted shampoo on a cat's coat

HANDLING DURING BATHING

Handle the cat firmly but gently. A cat does not like getting its fur wet and may try to scratch or bite. Talk to the cat to reassure it.

7 If the cat is not frightened, dry it thoroughly with a hairdryer. Hold the dryer at a safe distance, gently brushing the fur at the same time.

6 Carefully wipe around the cat's eyes, ears, and nose, using a soft, damp cloth *(see page 68)*.

Chapter 5

THE PROBLEM CAT

Badly behaved cats are a nuisance. Some normal feline behavior may be difficult for a human owner to understand and even more difficult to curb. Unacceptable feline behavior such as soiling and spraying inside the house, and aggression, may relate to stress and can often be tackled if the cause of the upset can be identified. Alternatively, you may find that your cat is extrovert or introvert by nature. Understanding and patience are essential if you arc living with a problem cat.

RECOGNIZING SIGNS OF STRESS

Even though a life in the wild would be more stressful for a cat than living with humans, a pet may suffer from stress if it is exposed to certain stimuli, or if its needs are not properly met. Anxiety can cause a cat to react in bizarre ways, such as soiling and spraying indoors, chewing wool, biting and scratching, and nervous grooming. There are different causes of stress, usually involving illness, pain, fear, or a change in the routine of the household due to the arrival of a new baby or pet. A cat may also suffer from stress following the loss of an owner or a change in living quarters.

ANXIOUS FELINE BEHAVIOR

The anxious cat
An anxious cat may appear nervous, crouching low on the ground. Other feline responses to stress include panting and shedding fur.

The body is tense

The pupils are dilated

Aggression (left)
A normally placid, affectionate cat may suddenly start to behave in an aggressive way, biting and scratching its owner. There is usually a good reason for this type of behavior. It may be a sign that the cat is sick and should be taken to a vet. A cat may also become aggressive or destructive through boredom or unresolved stress (see page 86).

The tail is held upright as the cat sprays the chair leg

Territory marking indoors (right)
A cat may spray inside the house if it is suffering from stress due to a change in its routine, or if another cat has been introduced into the home. The area must be washed with an odor neutralizer to remove the odor and discourage the cat from repeating the behavior.

House soiling

A cat that soils floors or furniture may be suffering from a urinary problem that requires veterinary treatment. If the cat is otherwise healthy, it may be a sign of stress. Do not scold or strike the cat. Provide it with a clean litter box until the problem is resolved. Deter the cat from soiling in the same place again by covering the spot with tin foil or plastic sheeting.

An anxious cat may lick and chew its fur

Nervous grooming *(above)*

There are cases of cats responding to stressful situations by overgrooming. The cat may continually lick and chew one particular area of its body for no apparent reason. This can lead to skin conditions such as dermatitis, eczema, and even baldness. A vet may treat the cat by prescribing tranquilizers to help while the stress is being resolved.

IDENTIFYING PROBLEMS

If there is no obvious reason for your cat's problem, consult a vet who may refer your pet to an animal behaviorist for treatment.

Chewing wool

Certain breeds of oriental cat, especially Siamese and Burmese, may sometimes obsessively chew wool and other types of fabric. Such cats may be reverting to infant behavior as a result of stress.

DEALING WITH UNWANTED BEHAVIOR

We need to recognize the the difference between normal but unwanted feline behavior and more serious problems, such as phobias. Some aspects of normal cat behavior can put a strain on your relationship with your pet, but you must remember that your cat is just following its natural instincts when it chooses a favorite plant for its toilet or scratches your best armchair. If you teach your pet boundaries and give it direction from the time it is a kitten, it will be less likely to behave in an undesirable way as an adult cat.

Never shout at or strike a cat; a firm "No" will usually stop it in its tracks. As a last resort, a quick squirt of water from a water pistol may stop a cat persisting with bad behavior.

UNWANTED FELINE BEHAVIOR

Digging up plants
A cat's habit of digging up the soil around plants (both indoors and out) when selecting a site for its toilet is a nuisance to many gardeners. If your cat selects a nearby garden for its toilet, you and your pet will soon become very unpopular with neighbors.

The cat dislikes the feel of the gravel

Remedy *(right)*
Garden plants can be surrounded with wire mesh or netting to discourage a cat from using a particular spot. Various odors, such as buried moth balls, may also act as deterrents. Probably the most effective way to stop a cat's gardening activities is to place sharp gravel around precious plants.

Fighting with other cats
An unneutered tomcat is likely to fight with other rival cats. An intact male cat's natural instinct is to defend its territory against other males and to seek out females to mate with. If you own such a cat and allow it to roam free outdoors, you can expect it to often come home battle-scarred from brawling.

Remedy *(above)*
Neutering a male cat makes it less aggressive toward other cats. It is likely to have a smaller territory to protect, stray less, and make a more affectionate pet *(see page 154)*.

Eating houseplants

Cats often like to nibble at the leaves of houseplants. A cat that is confined indoors may eat plants as a substitute for grass, which all cats like to chew on. Do not keep any plants that are toxic to cats in your home *(see page 167)*.

A cat may eat houseplants if it has no access to grass

(see page 167)

CAT SANCTUARY

Simple touches can enrich your cat's life and improve its behavior. Every feline needs a quiet place where it can sleep undisturbed.

Remedy *(right)*

Houseplants can be protected by putting an anti-chew agent on the leaves. If this does not work, try spraying the cat with a plant spray or water pistol (using only clean water) every time it misbehaves.

Scratching furnishings

A cat scratches furnishings not merely as a way of manicuring its claws, but also to mark the extent of its territory as a signal to other felines. The more confined or threatened a cat feels, the more likely it is to mark its home.

Remedy *(right)*

Think carefully when choosing curtains, carpets, and chairs. Some textured fabrics or rough wallpaper will be irresistible to a cat. Train your cat to use a scratching post *(see page 36)*.

A post is good for sharpening claws

(see page 36)

CARING FOR AN INTROVERT CAT

Cats are well known for their independent natures, but some individuals may be rather timid and withdrawn. The root of the problem usually lies in the way a cat was raised. A kitten should be brought up in a stimulating environment, in which it feels secure. It should be encouraged to investigate new objects and to interact with other cats. A kitten that is not used to being handled and that is deprived of human attention will grow up into a cat that is timid and wary of humans.

THE TIMID CAT

Wary of humans
A timid or nervous cat may have been mistreated or undersocialized when it was young. A sudden noise or the appearance of a stranger in the house is enough to to make it hide away in a corner.

The eyes are wary

The tail is held between the legs

Gentle reassurance (below)
Never reach for a timid cat; let it come to you in its own time. A cat often perceives any unwanted advance as aggression. Reassure the cat by speaking to it softly and, if it will allow it, gently stroking it at the same time. The cat may feel safer if it is on a table or raised surface above floor level – lure it there. Avoid making sudden movements or loud noises. Keep visitors away until the cat has gained confidence.

A secure refuge (above)
A timid cat needs a quiet refuge where it can retreat in times of stress. An enclosed cat bed may help it to overcome its nervousness.

THE DEPENDENT CAT

The ears are forward and alert

The mouth is open; this cat is very vocal

Demanding attention
Another type of introvert cat is completely reliant on its human owner and will probably follow you around looking for reassurance. A dependent cat will seek constant love and attention. It will probably cry when it wants to be picked up or when it wants to be fed, or sometimes simply because it wants attention.

The body is held upright, demanding attention

Making friends (*right*)
A dependent cat is likely to suffer from loneliness whenever it is separated from its owner. Provide it with a feline companion, and encourage it to be more independent by allowing it to explore and experience new situations.

Companionship (*above*)
A kitten may help encourage a dependent cat to be more outgoing and less reliant on its owners for amusement. The kitten will make an ideal companion for the older cat to play with if it is to be left alone for long periods, and will prevent it from getting bored or lonely. The younger the kitten, the more likely it is to be accepted by the adult cat (*see page 33*).

CARING FOR AN EXTROVERT CAT

A boisterous or extrovert cat can be quite a handful. It will require constant attention to keep it out of mischief. Most felines grow out of kittenish behavior, but an extrovert cat will stay lively and playful into adulthood. It is neither possible nor practical to train a cat in the same way as a dog. However, a kitten or young cat should be taught some basic discipline to prevent it from developing bad habits in later life.

THE AGGRESSIVE CAT

Biting and scratching
A cat may bite or scratch during play or when stroked. There is usually a reason for aggressive behavior. The cat may be sick, in pain, or overstimulated.

The ears are held back

The claws are out

The hind legs are used to kick

Tap the cat's nose gently with two fingers

Discipline *(left)*
Never hit or strike out at a cat. This will only make it nervous and cause it to run off and hide. However, you should scold a cat every time it misbehaves, using a firm, sharp tone of voice. A gentle tap on the cat's nose with two fingers may also be effective.

An extrovert cat needs toys for stimulation

Attention seeking
Most cats get all the stimulation they need by exploring their environment. A cat that is not given enough attention may become aggressive and destructive. Cats needs plenty of human contact and stimulation in the form of games and toys *(see pages 46–47)* to keep them amused. A feline companion may help, especially if a pet is left alone for long periods.

THE STRAYING CAT

Leaving home

An unneutered cat or one that is not getting the care and attention that it needs (for example, if it is left alone or fed at irregular times) may stray or desert the home altogether. A cat can survive very well without humans or, if it wants, find a new home. However, it may be picked up as a stray or become wary of humans and revert to a semi-feral state.

The eyes and ears are alert

The tail is held high

The stride is confident and purposeful

Keeping a cat confined

A cat that has a tendency to stray may need to be confined indoors for a short period. To prevent your cat from wandering too far from home, train it to come when you call it at feeding times. A cat should not be allowed to stay outdoors all night since this is a dangerous time.

A cat relies on its owner to provide it with food

Feeding times (*right*)

If a cat is fed at regular times in the morning and evening, this will ensure that it is not far from home at feeding times. Your relationship with your cat is based on the principle that you provide it with food. If this supply is withdrawn, a cat is likely to go off in search of a new home.

Chapter 6

YOUR CAT'S HEALTH

When you take a cat into your home, its health becomes your responsibility. Your vet will provide vaccinations against infectious diseases, as well as regular checkups and treatment for your cat if it should become sick. You should learn to keep a careful watch on your cat's health at home, so that you can recognize the first signs of illness. Disorders that affect a cat's eyes, ears, and coat are usually fairly obvious. If you notice any abnormalities in the appearance of your cat or any changes in its behavior, contact a vet immediately.

THE HEALTHY CAT

A healthy cat is a glorious sight. It is confident, alert, and interested in and aware of everything that is going on around it, even when it appears to be taking a quiet catnap. Assessing your cat's state of health by regularly examining it *(see pages 96–97)* and carefully observing its behavior is not difficult, but it does need to be done in a routine way so as not to miss any vital sign. A sick cat often does not show any symptoms, and you may not notice that there is anything wrong until it is too late for minor medical treatment.

It is best to look over your cat when it is fairly relaxed and, if possible, without it realizing what you are doing. If you know what to look for, a quick survey of your cat when you are grooming it or when it is sitting on your lap should tell you much about its condition.

A cat's behavior is usually the best indicator of whether it is healthy. If you notice any small changes, such as a loss of appetite, a marked decrease in levels of activity, or listlessness, do not hesitate to consult a vet immediately. If you are worried about any aspect of your cat's health or notice any type of unusual behavior, you can telephone the clinic first and ask the advice of the trained staff before you make an appointment for a consultation.

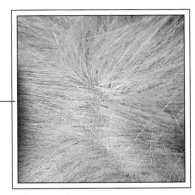

Skin and coat
A cat's coat should look sleek and glossy and be springy to the touch. The skin should be free of scratches or fight wounds, and there should be no signs of fleas or baldness.

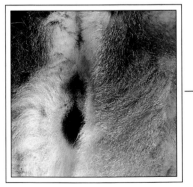

Rear
A cat will keep the area under its tail very clean. There should be no evidence of soreness or diarrhea.

Feline fitness
A healthy cat should have a good appetite and, when it wants, can be very active, moving with grace and agility. It should groom itself regularly and enjoy being petted and handled.

Ears

The outer part of a cat's ears tend to become dirty and should be gently cleaned once a week *(see page 69)*. The ears should be a healthy pink color inside, and there should be no signs of discharge or accumulation of dark-colored wax. Never poke anything into the ear canal.

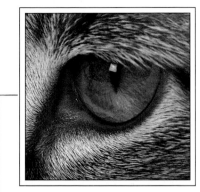

Eyes

A cat's eyes should be clear and bright and free of any discharge. If the third eyelid is showing, this is a sign that a cat is sick.

Nose

A cat's nose should feel soft and velvety and damp to the touch. The nostrils should be free of discharge and have no crusting on the surface. Consult a vet if a cat is sneezing continually, since this may be a sign of a respiratory virus.

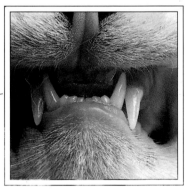

Mouth and teeth

Regular brushing will keep a cat's teeth clean and its breath free of smell. There should be no broken teeth, and the gums should be pale pink and free of inflammation.

SIGNS OF ILL HEALTH

The signs described below and opposite may be accompanied by changes in your cat's general behavior; these can often be the first indication that something is wrong. Your cat may spend more time sleeping, drink more than normal, be reluctant to play, or lose its appetite. It is difficult to tell whether your cat is in pain and which part of its body is affected; it may be restless, cry out, or just want to hide itself away. If you can say when your cat first showed signs of ill health, this will help the vet make a diagnosis.

EYE DISORDERS
(see page 105)
- Discharge from the eye
- Inflammation of the eyelid
- Change in the eye color
- Abnormal sensitivity to light
- Visible third eyelid
- Problems with vision

EAR DISORDERS
(see page 107)
- Discharge from the ear
- Dark brown wax in the ear
- Persistent scratching or rubbing of the ears
- Head shaking or holding head to one side
- Swelling of the ear flap
- Hearing problems

RESPIRATORY DISORDERS
(see page 109)
- Labored breathing
- Persistent sneezing
- Persistent coughing
- Discharge from the eyes and nose
- High temperature

MOUTH AND TOOTH DISORDERS
(see page 115)
- Drooling and pawing at the mouth
- Inflamed gums
- Missing, loose, or broken teeth
- Bad breath
- Difficulty in eating
- Loss of appetite

When to call a vet
Contact a vet immediately if your cat appears to be in pain or if it is obviously injured. Keep the telephone number of the clinic in a prominent place, so that you can find it easily in case of an emergency.

SKIN PARASITES
(see page 103)
- Persistent scratching
- Loss of hair
- Excessive grooming
- Biting at the skin and coat
- Signs of parasites in the coat

DIGESTIVE DISORDERS
(see page 111)
- Repeated vomiting
- Persistent diarrhea
- Loss of appetite
- Blood in the feces or vomit
- Persistent constipation

NERVOUS DISORDERS
(see page 121)
- Convulsions and fits
- Muscle spasms and tremors
- Partial or complete paralysis
- Staggering gait
- Acute skin irritation

SKIN AND COAT DISORDERS
(see page 101)
- Persistent scratching
- Excessive licking and grooming
- Biting at the skin and coat
- Swelling under the skin
- Bald patches in the coat
- Increased shedding of the hair

BLOOD AND HEART DISORDERS
(see page 123)
- Collapse or fainting
- Bluish discoloration of the gums
- Breathing difficulties
- Unwillingness to exercise
- Coughing while exercising

REPRODUCTIVE DISORDERS
(see page 117)
- Failure to breed
- Bleeding from the genitals
- Abnormal discharge from the vulva
- Swelling of the mammary glands
- Swelling of the testes

INTERNAL PARASITES
(see page 113)
- Worms passed in the feces
- Persistent diarrhea
- White "grains" visible on the rear
- Licking and rubbing of the behind
- Potbellied appearance
- Loss of weight

URINARY DISORDERS
(see page 119)
- Straining to pass urine
- Abnormal urination or incontinence
- Blood or excessive cloudiness in the urine
- Excessive thirst
- Persistent licking of the genitals

BONE, MUSCLE, AND JOINT DISORDERS
(see page 99)
- Lameness and limping
- Swelling around the affected area
- Tenderness when area is touched
- Reluctance to walk or jump
- Abnormal gait

DIAGNOSIS CHART

This flowchart is intended to be a rough guide for you to find out what is wrong with your cat. If your pet is showing any of these clinical symptoms, it may be the first sign of a health problem. Always contact a vet if you are in the slightest doubt about your cat's health.

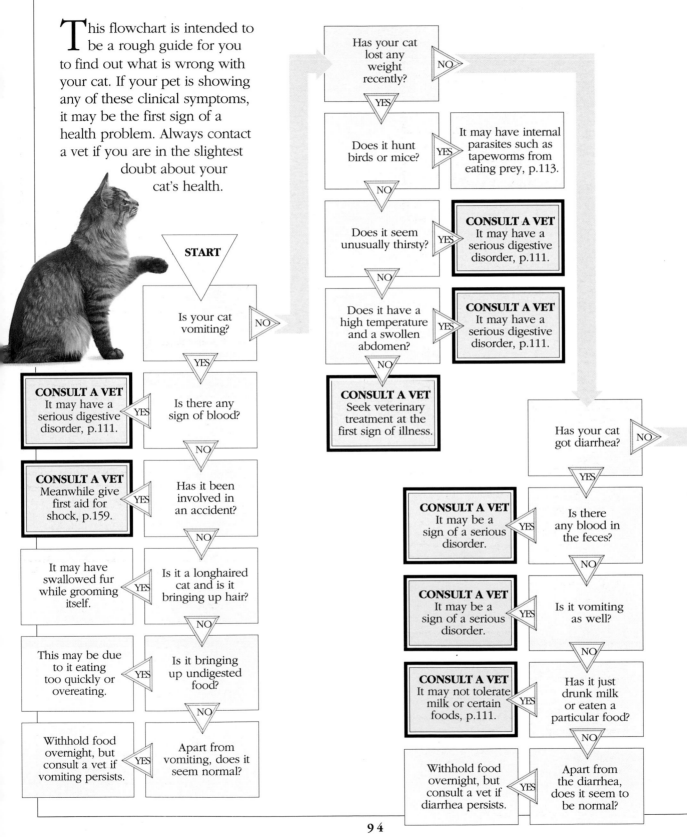

Has your cat lost any weight recently? NO

YES

Does it hunt birds or mice? YES → **It may have internal parasites such as tapeworms from eating prey, p.113.**

NO

Does it seem unusually thirsty? YES → **CONSULT A VET** It may have a serious digestive disorder, p.111.

NO

Does it have a high temperature and a swollen abdomen? YES → **CONSULT A VET** It may have a serious digestive disorder, p.111.

NO

CONSULT A VET Seek veterinary treatment at the first sign of illness.

START

Is your cat vomiting? NO

YES

CONSULT A VET It may have a serious digestive disorder, p.111. ← YES — **Is there any sign of blood?**

NO

CONSULT A VET Meanwhile give first aid for shock, p.159. ← YES — **Has it been involved in an accident?**

NO

It may have swallowed fur while grooming itself. ← YES — **Is it a longhaired cat and is it bringing up hair?**

NO

This may be due to it eating too quickly or overeating. ← YES — **Is it bringing up undigested food?**

NO

Withhold food overnight, but consult a vet if vomiting persists. ← YES — **Apart from vomiting, does it seem normal?**

Has your cat got diarrhea? NO

YES

CONSULT A VET It may be a sign of a serious disorder. ← YES — **Is there any blood in the feces?**

NO

CONSULT A VET It may be a sign of a serious disorder. ← YES — **Is it vomiting as well?**

NO

CONSULT A VET It may not tolerate milk or certain foods, p.111. ← YES — **Has it just drunk milk or eaten a particular food?**

NO

Withhold food overnight, but consult a vet if diarrhea persists. ← YES — **Apart from the diarrhea, does it seem to be normal?**

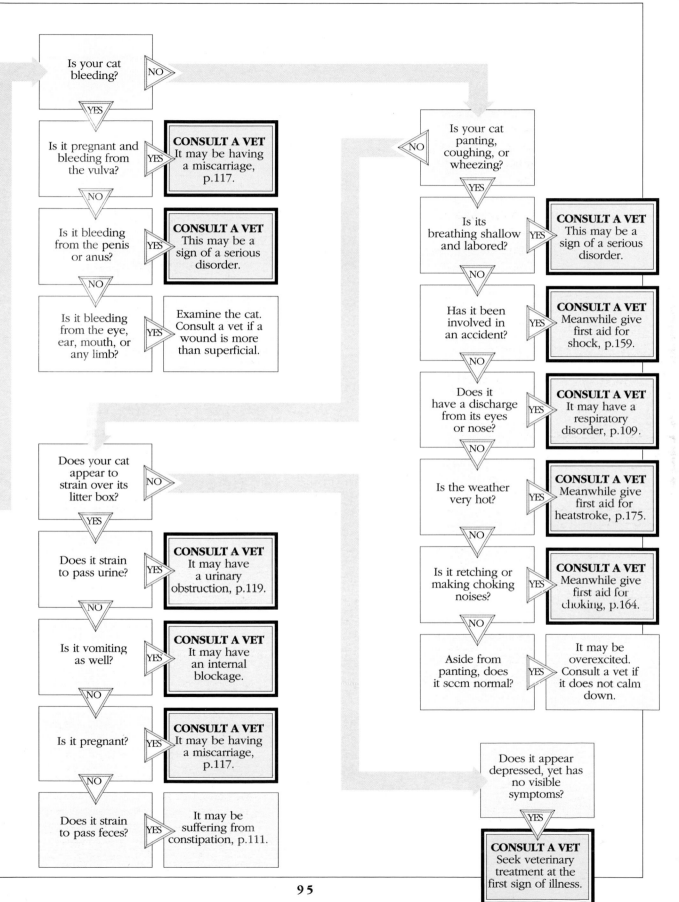

Is your cat bleeding? — NO

YES

Is it pregnant and bleeding from the vulva? — YES — **CONSULT A VET** It may be having a miscarriage, p.117.

NO

Is it bleeding from the penis or anus? — YES — **CONSULT A VET** This may be a sign of a serious disorder.

NO

Is it bleeding from the eye, ear, mouth, or any limb? — YES — Examine the cat. Consult a vet if a wound is more than superficial.

Does your cat appear to strain over its litter box? — NO

YES

Does it strain to pass urine? — YES — **CONSULT A VET** It may have a urinary obstruction, p.119.

NO

Is it vomiting as well? — YES — **CONSULT A VET** It may have an internal blockage.

NO

Is it pregnant? — YES — **CONSULT A VET** It may be having a miscarriage, p.117.

NO

Does it strain to pass feces? — YES — It may be suffering from constipation, p.111.

Is your cat panting, coughing, or wheezing? — NO

YES

Is its breathing shallow and labored? — YES — **CONSULT A VET** This may be a sign of a serious disorder.

NO

Has it been involved in an accident? — YES — **CONSULT A VET** Meanwhile give first aid for shock, p.159.

NO

Does it have a discharge from its eyes or nose? — YES — **CONSULT A VET** It may have a respiratory disorder, p.109.

NO

Is the weather very hot? — YES — **CONSULT A VET** Meanwhile give first aid for heatstroke, p.175.

NO

Is it retching or making choking noises? — YES — **CONSULT A VET** Meanwhile give first aid for choking, p.164.

NO

Aside from panting, does it seem normal? — YES — It may be overexcited. Consult a vet if it does not calm down.

Does it appear depressed, yet has no visible symptoms? — YES

CONSULT A VET Seek veterinary treatment at the first sign of illness.

EXAMINING A CAT

If you suspect that your cat is sick, a basic check on its bodily functions will be useful in assessing its condition. You can make such health checks a routine, beginning when the cat is very young. Regular examination has a number of benefits. It allows you to detect early changes in your cat's health, and makes it possible for you to give the vet a full report on any unusual signs that you have observed. Most important of all, it helps to reinforce the bond between you and your cat.

When subjecting your cat to examination, always be firm but gentle, and talk to it in a reassuring way. None of the techniques shown on these pages is difficult. They just require a little understanding of feline behavior and practice.

TAKING THE PULSE

1 Place the cat on a table or other raised surface. Make sure that the cat is as calm and relaxed as possible by talking to it in a soothing way.

2 The cat's pulse is best felt high up on the inside of the hind leg. You should always count the pulse beats for at least two separate minutes.

TAKING THE TEMPERATURE

1 First, shake the thermometer and lubricate it with petroleum jelly. Lift the cat's tail and insert the thermometer.

READING A THERMOMETER

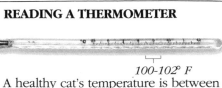

100-102° F

A healthy cat's temperature is between 100 and 102°F (38 and 39°C).

2 Carefully hold the thermometer in the cat's rectum for at least one minute. Remove and wipe it before reading.

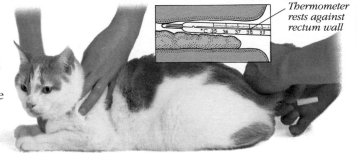

Thermometer rests against rectum wall

VITAL SIGNS

Normal pulse, temperature, and respiration rates are: pulse: 160–240 beats per minute; temperature: 100–102°F/38–39°C; respiration: 20–30 breaths per minute.

CHECKING BODY FUNCTIONS

Breathing
Listen to either the breaths out or the breaths in. Here the cat's breathing is being checked by a vet, with a stethoscope.

Abdomen
With the cat at ease, gently palpate the abdomen for any signs of swelling or tenderness. Use a gentle touch, since the cat may react if it is in pain.

Ears
Look into the ears but do not put things in them. Note any scratches to the outer ear, inflammation, or dark-colored wax, which may be a sign of ear mites.

Eyes
Look for discharges, inflammation, or signs of injury. Do not put any drops in a cat's eyes without consulting a vet, and never touch the eyeball itself.

Mouth
Open the cat's mouth and look for broken teeth, inflamed gums, or a buildup of dental deposits that may require scaling by a vet.

Claws
Gentle pressure on the cat's foot will unsheathe the claws. Note any broken or missing claws and any injuries to the soft web of skin between the cat's paw pads.

BONE, MUSCLE, AND JOINT DISORDERS

A cat's agility and elegance are made possible by its highly refined skeleton and the joints and muscles that make it work. Cats are seldom victims of muscle or joint disorders, although an elderly feline may suffer from inflammation of the joints and lameness, which require treatment by a vet. The most serious problems are bone fractures, joint sprains, and injuries from fighting. Always consult a vet for treatment of any serious injury, since the cat is likely to be suffering from severe shock.

Fractures
Although a cat's skeleton is very strong, fractures do occur as a result of accidents.

THE FELINE SKELETON

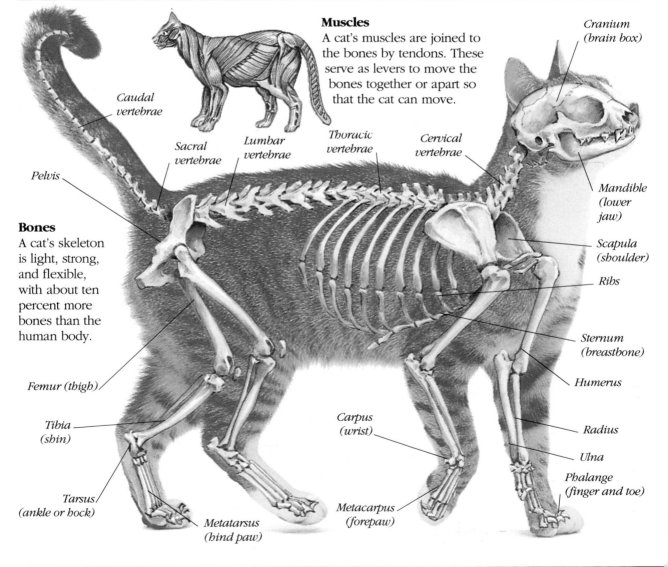

Muscles
A cat's muscles are joined to the bones by tendons. These serve as levers to move the bones together or apart so that the cat can move.

Bones
A cat's skeleton is light, strong, and flexible, with about ten percent more bones than the human body.

Caudal vertebrae

Sacral vertebrae

Lumbar vertebrae

Thoracic vertebrae

Cervical vertebrae

Cranium (brain box)

Pelvis

Mandible (lower jaw)

Scapula (shoulder)

Ribs

Sternum (breastbone)

Femur (thigh)

Humerus

Tibia (shin)

Carpus (wrist)

Radius

Ulna

Tarsus (ankle or hock)

Metatarsus (hind paw)

Metacarpus (forepaw)

Phalange (finger and toe)

BONE, MUSCLE, AND JOINT DISORDERS

Disorder	Description and signs	Action
Bone fractures	Most fractures are caused by traffic accidents or awkward falls. Broken bones are classified according to their severity. A simple fracture does not break through the skin, whereas in a compound fracture the bone is exposed. Fractures are associated with shock, blood loss, and internal injuries.	Consult a vet immediately for setting of the broken limb. Do not attempt to treat a fracture yourself by splinting the limb (see page 161).
Dislocation	A dislocated joint can be the result of a fall or other accident. The hip is the joint most commonly affected. Signs are a sudden pain with an inability to put weight on the limb.	Urgent veterinary treatment is needed. The vet will replace the joint in its socket under an anesthetic.
Bone infection	A deep fight wound may worsen and the infection spread to the bone. Signs of a bone infection include lameness, fever, swelling, and perhaps a discharge.	All serious bite wounds must be treated by a vet. Antibiotics may be prescribed to prevent infection.
Mineral deficiency	Kittens fed a diet of all muscle meat do not get enough minerals. This leads to poor bone development and stunted growth. The condition can also affect adult cats.	A vet can advise on the necessary corrections to the diet. Treatment may involve giving a mineral supplement.
Vitamin excess	Feeding a cat an excessive amount of foods high in vitamin A or D, or overdosing with a vitamin supplement can result in deformities of the spine.	The diet must be corrected at once. Do not give vitamin supplements unless recommended by a vet.
Cleft palate	A birth defect caused by a failure of the bones of the hard palate to develop fully (see page 115).	Surgery to correct the defect may sometimes be possible.
Arthritis	This condition sometimes occurs following a joint infection, dislocation, or trauma. It is most often due to a degeneration of the cartilage in joints as a result of old age. Signs include painful, stiff joints and lameness.	Consult a vet immediately if your cat shows any signs of lameness. Anti-inflammatory drugs may be prescribed to relieve the condition.
Sprains	Although muscle problems are rare, a sprain may sometimes occur when a tendon or ligament is stretched beyond its limits. The signs are swelling and a temporary lameness.	If there is any swelling of the limb, consult a vet immediately. Treat with cold compresses.

BONE FRACTURES

When bones break as the result of an accident, the surrounding tissues are likely to be damaged as well. The cat will probably be in severe shock, and the fractured limb will be swollen and painful due to internal bleeding and bruising. The bones must be immobilized for as long as it takes for them to heal properly. Cats make good subjects for treatment, since they take to cage rest and can cope with splints and pins. Even if a limb has to be amputated, a three-legged cat quickly learns to get around without difficulty.

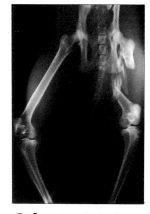

Before treatment
A radiograph shows the extent of injuries to a thigh bone. Although the femur is shattered into several pieces, it is not beyond repair.

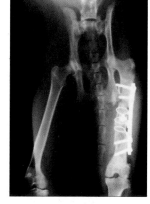

After treatment
Following surgery, the broken bone fragments have been realigned and immobilized. Healing usually takes several weeks.

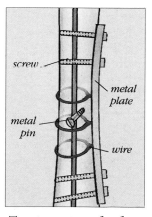

screw

metal plate

metal pin

wire

Treatment method
The bone fragments are carefully pieced together. They are immobilized using a combination of encircling wires, a steel plate, and some screws.

SKIN AND COAT DISORDERS

There are two types of skin disorder: parasitic and nonparasitic. External parasites such as fleas, lice, and ticks are very common in cats *(see pages 102–103)*. Other nonparasitic conditions that can affect the skin and coat are dermatitis, ringworm, stud tail, feline acne, tumors, and abscesses due to fight wounds. Most problems are not contagious and respond well to treatment. Ringworm, however, can be transmitted to other cats, and even to humans.

The main signs of skin disorders are irritation, inflammation and changes in the surrounding skin, and hair loss. They are not specific to any one ailment. Changes in the skin and coat can sometimes be an indication of a serious illness, and if a cat stops grooming itself this may be an early sign that it is sick.

Self-grooming
Meticulous grooming keeps skin and coat problems to a minimum.

ANATOMY OF THE SKIN

Layered protection
The skin helps to control a cat's temperature and to minimize water loss. The coat is made up of heavy guard hairs and finer secondary hairs, all joined to a system of muscle fibers that allow the hair to come erect and bristle, especially along the back and over the tail.

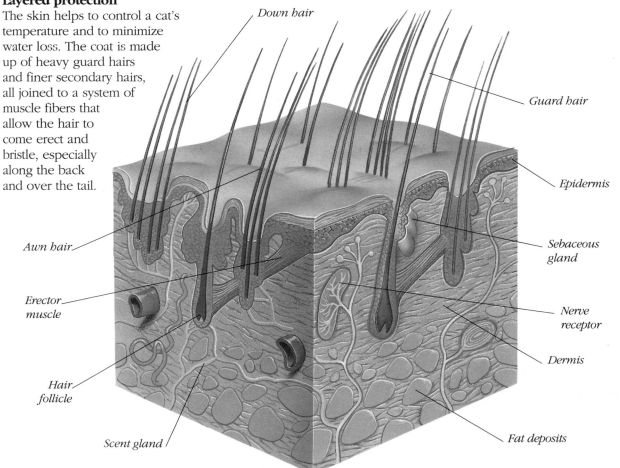

Down hair

Guard hair

Epidermis

Awn hair

Sebaceous gland

Erector muscle

Nerve receptor

Dermis

Hair follicle

Scent gland

Fat deposits

SKIN AND COAT DISORDERS

Disorder	Description and signs	Action
Abscess	This is a painful swelling that becomes infected and filled with pus. It is usually caused as a result of a fight wound (see page 169). The most common sites of abscesses are on the face and around the base of the tail.	Consult a vet if your cat has been bitten. The wound may become septic and require veterinary attention.
Dermatitis	Dermatitis is a term for several skin problems (commonly called eczema) that can cause inflammation and dry, scaly skin. Allergic dermatitis is caused by an allergy to certain foods (such as fish) or to flea dirt and may result in hair loss. Flea collar dermatitis is the result of a reaction to the insecticide in the collar and causes itching and redness. Solar dermatitis may affect the skin on the ears of white cats in sunny areas (see page 107).	Consult a vet. Treatment for dermatitis may involve giving the cat antibiotics and using anti-inflammatory or hormonal agents. Solar dermatitis may be controlled by applying protective suntan cream to the cat's ears. Flea collars should be removed at the first sign of irritation.
Ringworm	A skin infection caused by a parasitic fungus, not a worm. Signs of infection can be difficult to spot and vary from a few broken hairs on the face and ears to small, round patches of scaly skin on the cat's head, ears, paws, and back. A cat may carry the disease without showing any symptoms.	Ringworm can be treated with a variety of antiseptic creams and, in severe cases, antifungal drugs. Disinfection of all bedding is important because it is transmissible to humans (see page 125).
Tumor	A skin tumor is a swelling on or beneath the cat's skin and can be either benign or malignant – the latter means that it is cancerous. Cancerous growths usually grow very rapidly and cause bleeding and ulceration.	Examine any lump or growth that appears on your cat's skin. Consult a vet immediately if you are concerned.
Nervous grooming	Nervous licking or grooming of the coat may result in partial hair loss and sometimes dermatitis. This behavior may be caused by boredom or anxiety (see page 81).	Treatment involves identifying the reason for the stress. Tranquilizers or sedatives may be prescribed.
Feline acne	Acne on a cat's chin and lower lip is caused by blocked ducts leading to blackheads, pimples, and small abscesses forming on the skin.	Consult a vet if you notice any skin abnormality. Antibiotic treatment is sometimes needed.
Stud tail	This is an excessive secretion of oil from the sebaceous glands at the base of the tail. It commonly affects unneutered male cats and may cause staining on pale-colored cats.	Wash the coat with a safe shampoo, but consult a vet if it becomes infected or if there is irritation.
Hair loss	A neutered cat may suffer from hair loss on its hindquarters and abdomen. This may be due to a hormonal imbalance.	Consult a vet to identify the reason for the baldness.

RINGWORM

This skin infection is caused by a parasitic fungus, not a worm. It lives on the surface layers of the skin, causing inflammation and scratching. Signs of ringworm infection are usually seen as bald patches of scaly skin on the head, ears, paws, and back.

Some cats show no symptoms of the disease other than a few broken hairs. Diagnosis can be made using an ultraviolet lamp and by examining affected hairs under a microscope. Ringworm is highly contagious among cats living in a household and can be transmitted to other animals, even humans. Disinfection of baskets, bedding, and bowls during an outbreak is essential.

Treating ringworm (above)
The fur around the affected area may be clipped before treatment.

DERMATITIS

This is an inflammation of the skin and can be associated with many different factors. It is commonly caused by an allergic response, such as a reaction to flea dirt or certain foods. This results in an inflamed, itchy rash developing on the cat's skin. The condition can be aggravated by self-mutilation and infection. All skin conditions require careful investigation by a vet so that a proper diagnosis can be made. Procedures include various skin tests in which small samples of skin are removed and examined under a microscope.

SKIN PARASITES

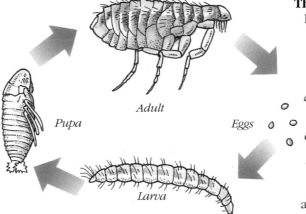

A variety of parasites can inhabit a cat's coat. Fleas are the most common cause of feline skin problems. Specks of "flea dirt" are easily seen in the coat, looking like large soot particles. Irritation can result from the fleas themselves or from sensitivity to their saliva or droppings. Fleas are involved in the life cycle of tapeworms and can lead to anemia.

Adult

Pupa

Eggs

Larva

The flea life cycle
Fleas flourish in a warm, humid environment. Eggs are laid on the cat's skin and on furniture. The larvae reach maturity and pupate in 7–10 days. The adult fleas emerge about 14 days later.

COMMON FELINE PARASITES

Flea Visible as pinhead-size, red-brown insects. Found around the neck and at the base of the tail.

Signs of infestation
Continuous or persistent scratching may be the first sign of infestation by parasites. Check the irritated area, then take appropriate action.

Ear mite The most common feline health problem, producing reddish-brown wax.

Fur mite Highly contagious. Visible as dry scales (dandruff) on the cat's back.

Tick Round, blood-sucking parasite. Must be removed carefully from skin.

Harvest mite Visible as tiny red dots on the cat's feet in autumn. Can be very irritating. Also known as "chiggers."

HUMAN INFECTION
Most parasites prefer not to live on humans. When they do get into clothing or onto skin, they are fairly easy to remove with sensible hygiene.

Louse Pinhead-size insect that feeds on the skin. Its white eggs (nits) may be visible on the cat's fur.

SKIN PARASITES

Parasite	Description and signs	Action
Fleas	The most common skin parasite. Fleas can carry tapeworm larvae *(see page 112)*. The presence of fleas is shown by persistent scratching and small black specks ("flea dirt") in the cat's coat. Some cats are allergic to flea bites due to a sensitivity to the flea's saliva.	Ask your vet to recommend a suitable insecticide spray or powder. Do not use a flea collar on a kitten or sick cat. Always follow the manufacturer's instructions very carefully.
Ticks	Sheep ticks are sometimes found on cats in country areas. They resemble small, blue-gray swellings and suck the cat's blood. A heavy infestation can sometimes cause anemia. There are some ticks in Australia that secrete a toxin that can result in paralysis (tick poisoning).	Dab the tick with alcohol and then remove it with tweezers. If the mouthparts remain in the skin, this can cause an abscess. Ask your vet to advise you on a suitable insecticide.
Lice	Lice are uncommon in healthy cats. They are found on the head and along the back and can be seen as white eggs (nits) attached to the cat's fur.	Consult a vet. In severe cases, the fur may need to be clipped, and the cat bathed in a suitable insecticide.
Mange mites	These minute skin parasites burrow into the cat's skin and cause a range of skin conditions, including inflammation and hair loss. The head mange mite affects the cat's head and neck. Other mites that can cause skin irritations are fur mites (also known as "walking dandruff"), harvest mites, and ear mites *(see page 107)*.	If you suspect that your cat has mites, consult a vet for identification and treatment of the skin parasites with a safe insecticide.
Fly strike	This condition especially affects longhaired cats with neglected or matted fur. Blowflies lay their eggs in the cat's fur, and the larvae burrow under the skin, causing skin damage and bacterial infections.	Consult a vet. The matted hair and damaged skin need to be cleaned with a safe antiseptic and treated with a suitable insecticide.
Bot flies	This type of fly is found mainly in parts of the United States. The bot fly grubs penetrate the cat's skin and may be seen as swellings on its neck, back, sides, and abdomen.	Veterinary treatment is needed if a cat has multiple swellings.

FLEA COLLARS

Collars are a useful aid to flea control, supplying continuous anti-flea medication. They should complement, rather than replace, normal household hygiene. Over-exposure to the medication in flea collars can sometimes cause skin irritation.

Safety *(right)*
Regularly remove flea collars to check for irritation.

TREATING PARASITES

The first rule in controlling fleas and other parasites is to maintain a high standard of hygiene in the cat's environment. No amount of dressings, powders, or sprays will be completely effective if this rule is not followed, since many parasites live or lay their eggs away from the cat and thrive in well-heated, modern homes. As well as treating the cat, you should also disinfect its bedding and all surrounding furnishings with a house spray to prevent parasites recurring. Cats are highly sensitive to a variety of insecticides, so you should ensure that preparations are always used as directed. A flea collar *(see page 38)* should have an elasticized section and should be replaced every few months to ensure its effectiveness. Do not put a flea collar on a cat unnecessarily, if you have already managed to eliminate fleas from the house.

Sprays *(left)*
Keep any sprays away from the eyes. A cat may be frightened of the noise.

EYE DISORDERS

Changes in the appearance of a cat's eyes, whether due to infection or injury, are usually very noticeable. The most common eye conditions affect the cat's outer eye and the conjunctiva (the membrane covering the eyeball). The third eyelid is an extra protection that is not normally visible in a healthy animal, but which may come across the eye if a cat is sick. Signs of problems to watch out for are discharge or watering, closure of the eye, and any cloudiness or change in color. Consult a vet if you notice any abnormality – if left untreated, many eye conditions can lead to impaired sight or even blindness. Most common eye disorders can be treated with antibiotic drops or ointments prescribed by a vet (see page 132).

Inspecting the eyes
A vet can examine the deeper parts of a cat's eyes using an ophthalmoscope.

HOW THE EYE WORKS

Pupil dilation
The cat's vertical pupil protects the retina from bright light and can adjust to different light levels.

Pupil in darkness

Pupil in bright light

The structure of the eye
Light passes through the cornea and the lens to the light-sensitive cells of the retina, where impulses are sent to the brain via the optic nerve. A cat's eyes are specially designed to collect the maximum amount of light.

Optic nerve

Vitreous humor

Retina

Lens

Upper eyelid

Aqueous humor

Cornea

Pupil

Lower eyelid

Iris

Conjunctiva

Suspensory ligaments

EYE DISORDERS

Disorder	Description and signs	Action
Conjunctivitis	This common disorder is an inflammation of the outer layer of the eye (conjunctiva). The eyes will look red and swollen, and there will be a discharge. One or both eyes may be affected. Conjunctivitis can be a symptom of a viral infection such as Feline respiratory disease (see page 109).	Consult the vet for an examination of the cat's eyes. Treatment will usually be in the form of antibiotic drops or ointment. Never use medicines intended for humans.
Corneal damage and ulceration	Injuries to the eyes and eyelids during fights are common and normally heal quickly. If the wound becomes infected, there may be ulceration and even penetration of the cornea.	Consult a vet immediately. Urgent treatment of corneal ulcers is essential to avoid complications.
Protrusion of the third eyelids	The inner eyelid in the corner of the eye is not normally visible, but it may come across to protect an injured eye. If both eyes are affected, this is a sign that the cat may be out of condition or suffering from a viral infection.	Urgent treatment is needed where there is any injury to a cat's eyes. A cat should always be examined by a vet if it is out of condition.
Keratitis	An inflammation of the cornea results in the eye becoming cloudy. Signs include watering and sensitivity.	Urgent treatment is needed to prevent the condition from deteriorating.
Cataracts	An opacity of the lens of the eye is sometimes a congenital condition, but it is more often associated with elderly or diabetic cats.	Careful veterinary assessment is needed. Surgery may be possible to restore vision if both eyes are affected.
Glaucoma	This serious condition occurs when there is an increase in pressure within the eyeball. As a result, the cornea becomes cloudy and the eyeball enlarges.	Any apparent enlargement or change in the eyes should receive prompt veterinary treatment.
Bulging eye	Severe bulging or even dislocation of the eyeball may occur following an accident or as the result of an eye tumor.	Emergency veterinary treatment is needed as soon as possible.
Retinal diseases	Degeneration of the light-sensitive cells at the back of the eye (retina) may be inherited or due to a dietary deficiency. This eye disorder results in sight loss and may eventually lead to blindness.	Urgent veterinary treatment is required for diagnosis and to prevent the condition from deteriorating.
Watery eyes	An overproduction of tears or blocked tear ducts may cause facial staining.	Usually an inherited defect, associated with Pedigree Longhairs (see page 133).

THE THIRD EYELIDS

Gentle pressure on a cat's eyeball will expose the tiny shutter at the corner. If these eyelids are visible, this can be a sign that a cat is out of condition or is suffering from diarrhea or worms. Exposure of the third eyelid on one side only may be due to an injury, fight wound, or object in the eye.

Third eyelid

Eyelids (left)
Consult a vet if the third eyelid is visible.

BLINDNESS

Severe eye conditions such as retinal diseases or cataracts can result in a loss of sight. Cats cope surprisingly well with failing sight brought on by old age, or even with the loss of an eye following an accident or trauma. In familiar surroundings, they soon learn to adjust their behavior by using their other senses to compensate.

You should consult a vet immediately if your cat appears to have a sudden loss of vision. This may not be apparent if you look at the cat's eyes, but you may notice it misjudging heights or bumping into furniture.

Eye test (left)
To test sight, cover one eye and move your finger toward the other one, making the cat blink. Or shine a flashlight in the eye to see the pupil reflex.

EAR DISORDERS

A cat's ears not only control its hearing, but its sense of balance, as well. Infections of the middle and inner ear can therefore cause problems with a cat's mobility, as well as with its hearing. The most common causes of infection are certain microorganisms, foreign bodies, and ear mites. The signs of ear disorders to watch for include persistent scratching, shaking of the head, twitching of the ears, discharge, and the presence of dark wax. Deafness can occur following an infection, but it is more often a congenital defect associated with cats with white coats. Old age usually results in some loss of hearing.

Examining the ears

A vet can inspect the lower part of the ear canal using an otoscope. Do not poke anything into a cat's ears.

HOW THE EAR WORKS

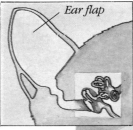

Ear flap

The outer ear
Sound waves are gathered by the sensitive outer ear and channeled to the ear drum.

Semicircular canals

The inner ear
The ear drum vibrates, moving the ossicles in the middle ear, which pass on the movement to the inner ear. The sound waves are translated into electrical impulses and conveyed to the brain.

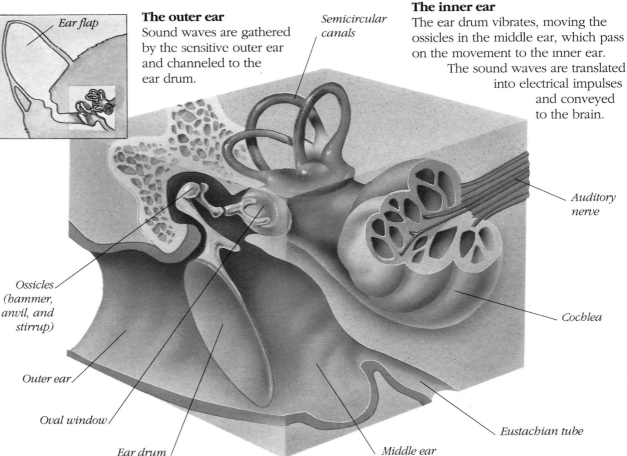

Auditory nerve

Ossicles (hammer, anvil, and stirrup)

Cochlea

Outer ear

Oval window

Eustachian tube

Ear drum

Middle ear

EAR DISORDERS

Disorder	Description and signs	Action
Ear mites	Mite infestation is very common in cats (especially in kittens). Tiny mites live in the ear canal and can cause irritation if they are present in large numbers. Signs of ear mites include persistent scratching and the accumulation of dark brown, pungent wax in the ears.	An examination of the cat's ears with an otoscope can confirm the presence of ear mites. All cats and dogs in the household will need to be treated with ear drops *(see page 133)*.
Ear infection	An inflammation of the ear canal can be caused by the presence of a foreign body, fungus, or bacteria in the ear. The cat will scratch the inflamed ear, leading to infection and sometimes a discharge.	Consult a vet for examination of the cat's ears. Treatment will usually involve administering ear drops *(see page 133)*.
Middle and inner ear infections	If an infection spreads to the middle or inner ear, it can result in damage to a cat's hearing. Signs of this disorder include loss of hearing and sense of balance. An affected cat may tilt its head to one side.	Prompt veterinary treatment with a course of antibiotics is usually needed. Delay may result in permanent damage to the cat's hearing.
Blood blister (hematoma)	Fighting or constant scratching may rupture blood vessels in the ear flap, producing a large blood blister. This is not painful, but it will cause irritation and the cat may continue to scratch and paw at it.	Consult a vet, who will drain the fluid from the ear. If the blood blister is left untreated, this may lead to scarring and a "cauliflower ear."
Sunburn	Pale-colored cats living in sunny areas, such as Florida, are prone to sunburn on their ear tips because of the lack of protective pigment in the skin *(see page 173)*. In time, skin damage may lead to cancerous growth and to the cat's ear becoming thickened and inflamed.	The cat should be kept indoors during the sunniest part of the day. A sunblock cream may provide some protection. Amputation of the ear tips is the only treatment for cancer.
Deafness	Loss of hearing may be the result of old age, middle ear infections, head injuries, or the ear canal becoming blocked with wax. Some cats are deaf from birth, especially some white cats with blue eyes *(see page 133)*.	A thorough veterinary examination is required where deafness is suspected.
Foreign bodies	Foreign bodies, such as grass seeds, can sometimes get caught in a cat's ears and may cause irritation and eventually lead to infection *(see above)*.	Consult a vet if the foreign body is not visible and cannot be easily removed *(see page 165)*.

EAR MITES

Most cats harbor some ear mites, but they usually only cause health problems if they are present in large numbers. The tiny mites feed on the delicate lining of the ear canal, causing irritation and the production of brown wax. This makes the cat scratch or shake its ears, thereby causing inflammation. Early veterinary attention is vital to make sure that any ear infection does not spread to the inner ear and affect the cat's centers of hearing and balance. It is important to keep your cat's ears clean and check regularly for signs of irritation or infection.

Ear mites are very contagious, so always treat both ears and treat all animals in the household.

Signs of mites (above)
Persistent scratching and head shaking are signs of mites.

EAR INJURIES

Because of their exposed position, a cat's ears are very prone to being bitten, torn, or scratched during fights. Such injuries can become infected if the wound is deep and may require veterinary treatment. Violent or persistent scratching may sometimes rupture blood vessels on the ear flap, producing a blood blister. Although this is not painful, it will irritate the cat, which will continue to scratch it. A vet can drain the fluid from the ear and support it, so it can heal in its correct shape. The ears of white cats are prone to damage from both frostbite *(see page 173)* and sunburn – the latter can lead to cancerous growth.

RESPIRATORY DISORDERS

Most respiratory illnesses that affect cats are due to infections by bacteria or viruses, and the upper respiratory tract is usually affected. Although the majority of conditions are mild and respond to careful nursing, they can become serious if neglected. Like human beings, cats can sometimes suffer from colds and occasional sneezing, coughing, and wheezing. Signs of respiratory disorders include breathing difficulties and discharge from the eyes and nose. A sick cat's breathing may be deep and labored or rapid and shallow. Coughs may be fluid and chesty or dry and harsh. It is important to get prompt veterinary help if your cat is showing any sign of illness, in order to prevent the condition from becoming chronic or life-threatening.

Listening to breathing
A vet can listen to a cat's breathing with a stethoscope. Radiographs may also help with the diagnosis.

THE RESPIRATORY SYSTEM

Breathing
Air is drawn into the cat's lungs through the nasal passage, which filters and warms it. The air passes down the trachea into the bronchi and the lungs, where the oxygen is absorbed by the blood and taken around the body.

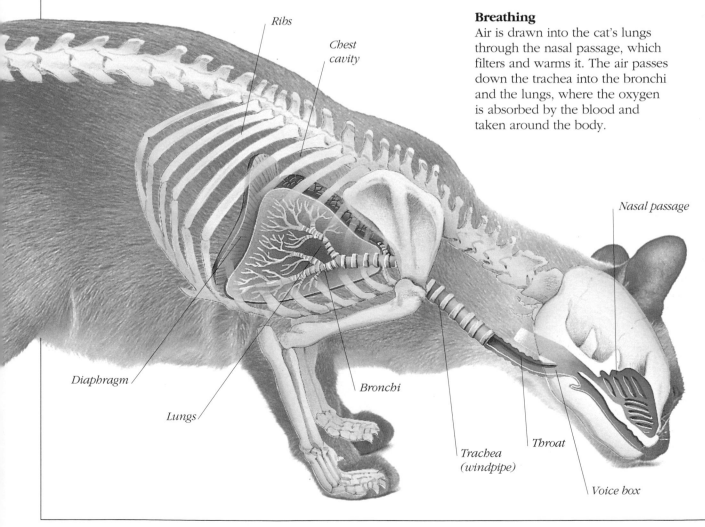

Ribs

Chest cavity

Nasal passage

Diaphragm

Lungs

Bronchi

Trachea (windpipe)

Throat

Voice box

RESPIRATORY DISORDERS

Disorder	Description and signs	Action
Feline respiratory disease ("cat flu")	The two most common respiratory viruses are Feline Viral Rhinotracheitis (FVR) and Feline Calici Virus (FCV). FVR is usually the more serious disease. The main sign of FVR is a watery discharge from the eyes and nose which becomes thicker as the disease progresses. A cat with FCV may also have a runny nose and eyes, and it will typically have ulcers on its tongue and mouth.	Prevention of FVR and FCV by vaccination is essential. Antibiotics may reduce the severity of the disease's effects, but much depends on the cat's immune system being able to fight off the virus. Recovery is often due to careful home nursing.
Pneumonia	A lung infection may follow severe respiratory diseases. Fever, difficulty in breathing, nasal discharge, and a cough are often associated with pneumonia.	Urgent veterinary treatment is needed. Careful nursing and cage rest are both an important part of the treatment.
Bronchitis	This condition usually accompanies other respiratory diseases. It is caused by an inflammation of the air tubes (bronchi) that link the windpipe to the lungs. Persistent coughing is the main symptom.	Urgent veterinary treatment is needed. Careful nursing and cage rest are both an important part of the treatment.
Pleurisy	A bacterial infection may lead to an inflammation of the layer covering the lungs (pleura). This causes a buildup of fluid in the chest cavity that makes breathing difficult.	Urgent veterinary treatment is needed. The fluid in the chest cavity may need to be drained.
Asthma	An allergic sensitivity can sometimes bring on an asthma attack. It is characterized by a sudden difficulty in breathing and wheezing and coughing.	Urgent veterinary treatment is needed to ease breathing and prevent repeated asthma attacks.
Chlamydial disease	This is caused by bacteria that produce signs similar to Feline respiratory disease *(see above)*.	A vaccine may give some protection against the disease.
Nasal discharge	A watery discharge from the nose and eyes is a sign of several infections. If the discharge is accompanied by sneezing and sniffling, the irritation may be due to an infection of the nasal cavities.	Consult a vet for examination and diagnosis of the infection.
Lungworm	This tiny parasite may be found in the lungs of cats in rural areas. Severely affected animals may have a dry cough.	A vet can prescribe drugs to treat the lungworm parasite.

LUNGWORM

The most common lung parasite that can infect cats is the lungworm. The signs of infection are usually mild, and most cats show no symptoms at all. A few, however, may develop a persistent dry cough. The lungworm life cycle is complicated, since it involves a snail or slug, as well as a rodent or bird, before it matures into an adult in a cat. An infected cat can often cough up parasites and get rid of them, but drugs are also available. In parts of North America tiny lung flukes can also infest cats.

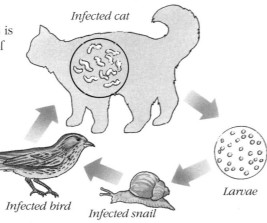

Infected cat

Larvae

Infected bird

Infected snail

Lungworm life cycle *(above)*
Larvae are eaten by a snail or slug, which, in turn, is swallowed by a bird or rodent. When this host is eaten by a cat the cycle is completed.

CAT FLU

The term "cat flu" is misleading, since there are several different viruses known by this name. Cats should be vaccinated against the main two feline respiratory viruses, Feline Calici Virus and Feline Viral Rhinotracheitis. However, other viruses exist for which there is no vaccine. The signs of all these infections are similar. An infected cat will have a runny nose and eyes, and may be sneezing or coughing. Cat flu can be serious, so it is best to consult a vet if your cat is showing any signs of illness. Telephone the clinic first, so that any necessary precautions can be taken to prevent the infection from spreading to other cats.

DIGESTIVE DISORDERS

Nutrients are broken down and used in a variety of ways to make a cat function properly. The digestive system is the center of this mechanism, converting food eaten by a cat to energy. The most common problems affecting the digestive system are vomiting, diarrhea, constipation, and appetite and weight loss. A cat may stop eating because it feels ill or has difficulty swallowing. Or it may eat too much, for a variety of reasons. Food may be vomited immediately after eating or only partly digested. A cat may show signs of excessive thirst or of constipation or diarrhea. Watch the symptoms carefully, since such health problems may require immediate medical attention.

Careful feeding
This is a cat's best protection against major diseases.

THE DIGESTIVE SYSTEM

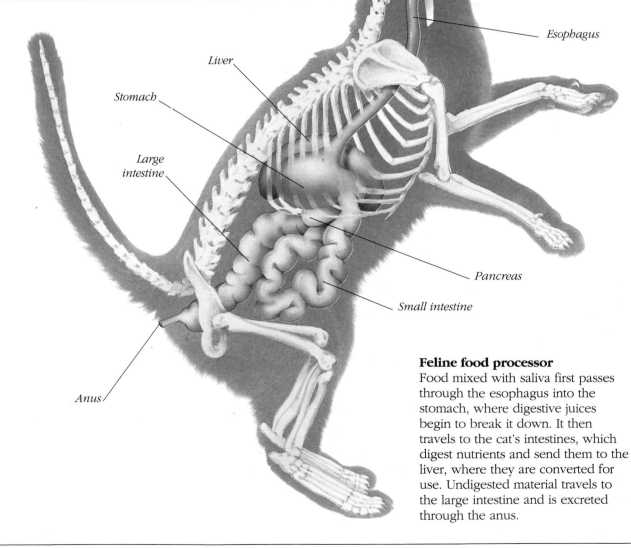

Mouth

Esophagus

Liver

Stomach

Large intestine

Pancreas

Small intestine

Anus

Feline food processor
Food mixed with saliva first passes through the esophagus into the stomach, where digestive juices begin to break it down. It then travels to the cat's intestines, which digest nutrients and send them to the liver, where they are converted for use. Undigested material travels to the large intestine and is excreted through the anus.

DIGESTIVE DISORDERS

Disorder	Description and signs	Action
Feline Infectious Enteritis (FIE), also known as Feline Panleukopenia	This widespread viral disease is highly contagious. It is spread by direct or indirect contact with an infected cat. FIE develops rapidly, so that in severe cases young kittens may die before a diagnosis can be made. The virus attacks the gut and the white blood cells. The main signs are depression, loss of appetite, and persistent vomiting and diarrhea.	Vaccination is effective in protecting a cat against FIE infection (see page 53). Early diagnosis and isolation of an infected cat is important to stop the disease from spreading. Careful nursing is essential to prevent dehydration.
Feline Infectious Peritonitis (FIP)	This virus primarily causes an infection of the abdominal cavity, but it also affects the liver, kidneys, nervous system, and brain. FIP mainly attacks cats under three years of age; older cats are more resistant. The main signs are loss of appetite, fever, weight loss, and a swollen abdomen.	Consult your vet on the availability of a vaccine. An infected cat must be isolated to prevent the disease from spreading to other cats. Treatment is not usually effective.
Vomiting	It is normal for a healthy cat to vomit occasionally, for example after eating grass or when getting rid of hairballs. Severe vomiting, abdominal pain, and excessive thirst indicate a serious digestive disorder that may be caused by a cat ingesting an irritant or contaminated food.	Vomiting or regurgitation of food may be due to several reasons. Consult a vet if the vomiting is severe or if it persists for more than 24 hours.
Diarrhea	Mild diarrhea may be caused by stress or a change in diet, but if the symptoms persist it may suggest a bacterial or viral infection. Diarrhea accompanied by vomiting or blood in the feces is a sign of a serious disorder.	Consult a vet if the diarrhea persists for longer than 24 hours or if there is any blood in the feces. Do not allow the cat to become dehydrated.
Liver disease	The liver may be damaged as a result of a viral disease or ingesting a poison. Signs of liver malfunction may include vomiting, diarrhea, excessive thirst, and abdominal pain.	Consult a vet immediately. Diagnosis can be aided by analysis of blood, urine, and fecal samples.
Diabetes	This condition is due to the inadequate production of insulin by the pancreas. Early signs are frequent urination, excessive thirst, increased appetite, and unexplained weight loss.	Treatment involves careful dietary control and, in some cases, daily injections of insulin.
Dietary sensitivity	Some oriental cats are unable to digest the sugar in milk, and this may cause diarrhea and vomiting. Other foods that may cause allergic reactions include fish and eggs.	A full veterinary examination is required to determine the cause of the sensitivity when it is not known.
Constipation	A cat should have a bowel movement at least once a day. Elderly cats, particularly longhaired types, are the most likely to suffer from a blockage in the bowel due to constipation.	Treat the cat with liquid paraffin by mouth. If there is no movement after two days, seek veterinary treatment.

DIARRHEA AND VOMITING

Cats vomit fairly readily as a means of protecting themselves against harmful substances. Anything more than occasional vomiting should be investigated by a vet, since it may indicate a serious problem. Diarrhea can be very debilitating and requires prompt veterinary attention, especially if the cat is vomiting or if blood is present. If not treated, severe diarrhea and vomiting can lead to collapse and even death through rapid dehydration. Such symptoms may be due to poisoning or Feline Infectious Enteritis, both of which need immediate veterinary treatment.

Examination (above)
A vet gently feels the abdomen for signs of swelling.

REFUSING TO EAT

Tempting a sick cat to eat is a delicate task. Try warming small amounts of a favorite food to body temperature and feeding several times daily.

Appetite loss (above)
Always consult a vet if a cat refuses food for more than 24 hours.

INTERNAL PARASITES

Parasites do not cause a cat much discomfort except when they are present in large numbers, but your cat is better off without them. The most common feline parasites are the worms that infest the intestinal tract, but there are also flukes, lungworms, heartworms, and protozoan organisms such as *Toxoplasma (see page 125).*

Many parasites spend their immature stages in another host, such as a rodent, flea, or bird, which must be eaten by a cat in order for the parasite to complete its life cycle.

Young cats are most at risk from parasitic infections, so it is essential to worm kittens from as early as four weeks old.

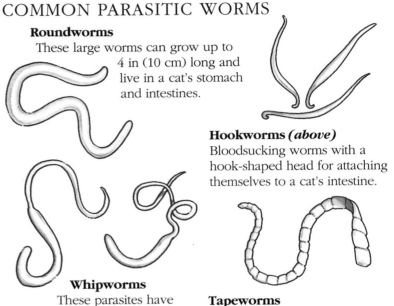

COMMON PARASITIC WORMS

Roundworms
These large worms can grow up to 4 in (10 cm) long and live in a cat's stomach and intestines.

Hookworms (above)
Bloodsucking worms with a hook-shaped head for attaching themselves to a cat's intestine.

Whipworms
These parasites have the appearance of a whip and live in the large intestine.

Tapeworms
Flat, segmented worms that attach themselves to a cat's intestine.

LIFE CYCLES OF COMMON PARASITES

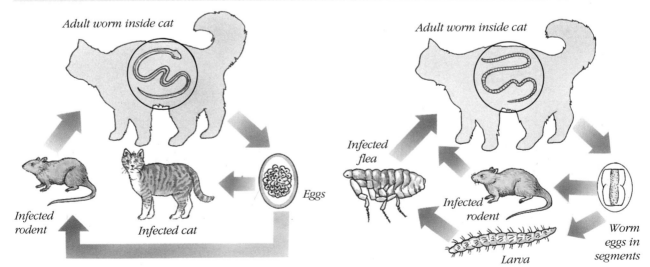

The roundworm life cycle
The adult worm lives in the cat's intestinal tract. It lays eggs that pass in the cat's feces, and the eggs may then be eaten by a rodent. Cats are infected by direct contact with the eggs, perhaps while grooming, or by eating a secondary host.

The tapeworm life cycle
The adult tapeworm sheds segments full of eggs, which pass in the feces. The eggs may then be eaten by a rodent or bird, and develop into larvae. The life cycle is completed when this host is eaten by a cat. Larvae can also be transmitted by fleas.

INTERNAL PARASITES

Parasite	Description and signs	Action
Roundworms	Roundworms live in the stomach and intestines and feed on digested food in a cat's gut. An adult cat may show no signs of having worms, but occasionally mature worms may be passed, or eggs may be detectable in the feces. Kittens can be infected via their mother's milk and become seriously weakened. Symptoms of a severe roundworm infestation include diarrhea, constipation, anemia, a potbellied appearance, and a loss of weight and condition.	Consult a vet, who can advise you on a suitable roundworm treatment. It is important that kittens and pregnant queens should be treated with worming tablets. Cats that hunt should be treated routinely two or three times a year.
Tapeworms	Tapeworms are most often found in adult cats. The worm has a long, segmented body and attaches itself to the intestine wall. The segments containing eggs are passed with the cat's feces, sometimes becoming stuck to the fur under the tail and drying out to resemble grains of rice. The shedding of segments may cause irritation, and the cat will lick its behind.	A vet can prescribe an appropriate tapeworm treatment. Flea control is also essential to prevent reinfection, since fleas can be intermediate hosts for certain species of tapeworm.
Hookworms	Bloodsucking hookworms are found in parts of North America. They live in the small intestine and can be passed to unborn kittens. Signs are diarrhea and weight loss.	A vet can prescribe an appropriate hookworm treatment. Strict hygiene measures are also recommended.
Threadworms and whipworms	Tiny threadworms and whipworms live in the gut and can infect cats in parts of North America and Australia. Signs may include diarrhea, but these worms rarely cause illness.	A vet can prescribe an appropriate worming treatment.
Flukes	Flukes are rarely found in cats, but these flatworms can sometimes infest the small intestine and liver in North America. They are caused by a cat eating infected raw fish. Signs include digestive upsets, and sometimes anemia.	A diagnosis by a vet is required to confirm a fluke infestation. Treatment is not always effective, and preventive measures are very important.
Lungworms	These tiny parasites sometimes infest a cat's lungs and can cause respiratory disease *(see page 109)*.	Consult a vet for treatment with a safe deworming drug.
Heartworms	Cats in some countries are infected by worms that live in the heart *(see page 123)*.	Consult a vet for treatment with a safe deworming drug.

PREVENTING INFESTATION

Discuss a worming program with a vet as soon as you get your cat. Maintaining hygiene standards around the home and keeping your cat free of external parasites, such as fleas, will also reduce the numbers of internal ones. Kittens should be treated from about four weeks old, and if worms and eggs are found in the feces, a course of treatment should be prescribed. Adult cats, particularly those that hunt prey and are allowed to roam freely, should be checked for worms at least twice a year.

Even though it may not be possible to prevent your cat from eating prey, you can reduce the risks of infestation by keeping its indoor environment unhospitable to parasite carriers such as mice and fleas. When you spray or dust your cat with insecticide, treat its bedding as well. Do not use any rodent poisons in the house, since they can be extremely toxic to cats *(see page 167)*.

Worming *(left)*
Try concealing a worming tablet in a small piece of food.

TREATMENT

There are many different worming preparations. It is important to obtain the correct remedy for the type of parasite infesting your cat. Worming medicine may be given in the form of a paste, which can be added to food or given directly by mouth. When giving pills, make sure that your pet swallows them and does not spit them out. Some pills may be only for roundworms, while others may kill a variety of parasites.

Pills for roundworm.

Pills for tapeworm.

MOUTH AND TOOTH DISORDERS

The cat's mouth and teeth are adapted to their role of hunting and catching prey, while the tongue is equipped with hooked, abrasive papillae used for grooming. Damage or inflammation to a cat's mouth, teeth, gums, palate, or tongue can make it difficult for it to eat, and it may be unable to groom itself. Eventually, the animal's life is endangered if action is not taken in good time.

Cats do not often get cavities in their teeth, but bacteria and debris may sometimes build up on the tooth surface to form plaque, and when mixed with minerals in the saliva, this hardens into tartar or "calculus." If not treated, gingivitis may result, followed by recession of the gums and the loss of teeth. There are a number of microorganisms, especially those associated with Feline respiratory disease or "cat flu" *(see page 109)*, that cause mouth ulcers. Occasionally, objects like fish bones can become lodged in the mouth and must be removed *(see page 164)*.

Carnivore
Although a cat's teeth are not very prone to decay, they benefit from regular cleaning. This is especially the case with older cats.

THE CAT'S TEETH

Feline fangs
Adult cats have 30 teeth, shaped for cutting and tearing meat, rather than for grinding or chewing. The carnassial teeth are adapted for slicing through flesh. A kitten gets its milk teeth at about 14 days old, and loses these to adult teeth at four to six months old.

THE SKULL
A cat has an immobile upper jaw, the maxilla, and a hinged lower jaw called the mandible, which consists of a vertical and a horizontal part.

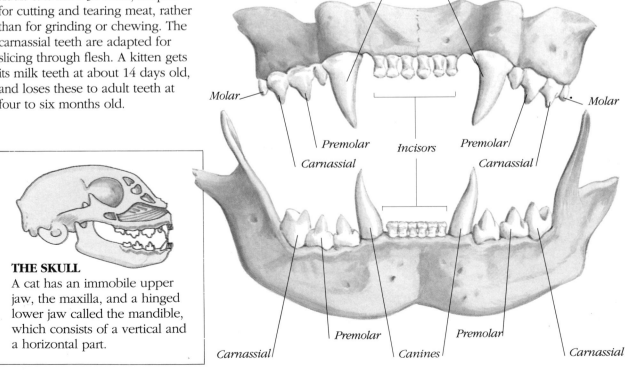

Canines

Molar

Molar

Premolar

Incisors

Premolar

Carnassial

Carnassial

Carnassial

Premolar

Premolar

Canines

Carnassial

MOUTH AND TOOTH DISORDERS

Disorder	Description and signs	Action
Cleft palate	Kittens are sometimes born with the two sides of the hard palate at the roof of the mouth not properly joined. Affected kittens will not be able to suckle milk properly.	Surgery to repair the hard palate may sometimes be possible.
Dental problems	Dental problems are common in older cats. The deposition of plaque on the tooth surface leads to brownish-yellow tartar ("calculus") forming on the teeth. This results in food being trapped, which causes inflammation of the gums (gingivitis). If the infection invades the tooth socket (periodontitis), the tooth will become loose or an abscess may form. A cat with dental problems may have bad breath, and it may experience difficulty in eating and paw at its mouth.	Regular brushing of your cat's teeth with a toothbrush helps prevent the buildup of plaque. If there is extensive tartar or a cat is very uncooperative, a vet can descale the teeth under an anesthetic, using an ultrasonic scaler.
Gingivitis	An inflammation of a cat's gums is the first sign of dental problems and is usually associated with a buildup of tartar on the teeth. Gingivitis may start as a dark red line bordering the teeth, but if it is left untreated the gums will become sore and ulceration may occur. A cat with gum disease may have bad breath, drool, and experience difficulty in chewing food.	Consult a vet if you notice any redness around a cat's mouth and gums. Regular brushing of a cat's teeth will help to keep the gums healthy.
Mouth infection	Stomatitis is an inflammation of the mouth lining. It may result from a foreign body in the mouth, a viral disease, or dental problems. An affected cat will have difficulty in eating, and the inside of the mouth will appear reddened.	Treatment depends on the cause of the infection. A vet will be able to identify the underlying cause.
"Rodent ulcer"	A "rodent ulcer" is a slowly enlarging sore or swelling on a cat's upper lip.	Consult a vet for treatment. "Rodent ulcers" tend to recur if the treatment is stopped too soon.
Salivary cyst	If the salivary glands or ducts that carry the saliva to the mouth become blocked, the result may be the formation of a salivary cyst (ranula) under the tongue.	Prompt veterinary treatment to drain the cyst is required since the cat will be unable to eat.
Mouth ulcers	Ulcers on a cat's tongue and gums are sometimes caused by Feline respiratory disease (see page 109) or kidney disease.	Consult a vet for an examination to determine the underlying cause.

GUM DISEASE

An inflammation of the gums is known as gingivitis. This is most commonly associated with an accumulation of tartar or "calculus" on the teeth, but can also indicate an internal disease if it is very severe. Health problems such as kidney disease (see page 119) and Feline Immunodeficiency Virus (see page 123) are often associated with inflammation of the gums. When an infection becomes established, the gums will recede, and in time the teeth will become loose in their sockets. Occasionally, a cat may have bad breath without any visible changes in its mouth. All clinical signs must be investigated by a vet, since they can lead to your cat losing its teeth or being unable to eat. Gum disease may be prevented by feeding your cat a sensible diet. A cat fed on soft food alone is especially prone to dental problems. Meat chunks or dry food in the diet will provide a cat with something to chew and help remove debris.

Gingivitis (above)
A dark red line along the gums is a sign of infection.

CLEANING TEETH

Tartar buildup can be retarded by cleaning a cat's teeth regularly. You may need someone to hold the cat steady while you brush its teeth using a special toothpaste or a weak saline solution (see page 69).

Brushing (above)
While the upper lip is held back, the back teeth can be brushed.

REPRODUCTIVE DISORDERS

Since a large number of male and female cats are neutered *(see pages 154–155)*, problems with the reproductive system are fairly uncommon. Most intact cats are very fertile and experience no difficulty in producing offspring, but there are disorders that can prevent queens from conceiving, or males from producing sperm.

There is no equivalent of the human menopause in cats. Reproductive activity does slow down as they grow older, but they can still reproduce and give birth at an advanced age.

Tumors of the testes are rare, but mammary tumors are fairly common. They usually occur after the cat is ten years old and need urgent attention. There is no evidence that having a litter of kittens before being neutered is good for a queen. Neutering will prevent the development of tumors if carried out before one year of age. Males with one or both testicles undescended are best castrated, since the condition is inherited.

Ultrasound scans
Ultrasound scans can be used to help monitor pregnancy in cats, just as in humans.

THE REPRODUCTIVE ORGANS

The male
The testes produce sperm that travel down the spermatic cord to the urethra. The penis is equipped with spines that trigger ovulation.

The female *(below)*
The female cat comes into heat, or "estrus," when the brain signals the pituitary gland to release a hormone that causes the ovaries to produce eggs. Another hormone causes behavioral changes, such as "calling" *(see page 144)*.

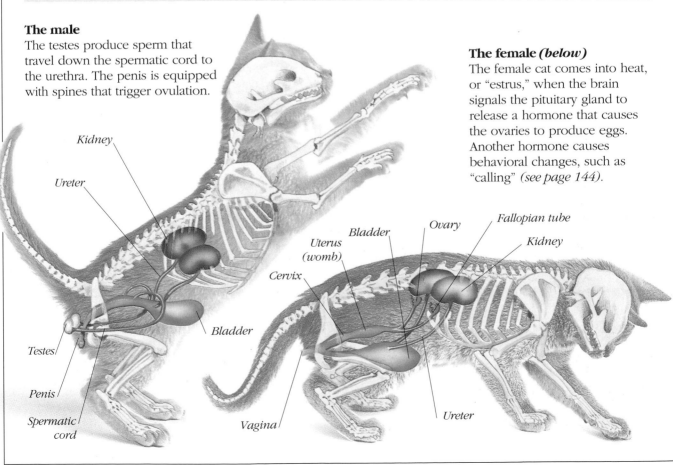

Kidney

Ureter

Testes

Penis

Spermatic cord

Bladder

Uterus (womb)

Cervix

Bladder

Ovary

Fallopian tube

Kidney

Vagina

Ureter

REPRODUCTIVE DISORDERS

Disorder	Description and signs	Action
Female infertility	If a female cat fails to conceive after mating, this may be due to a number of factors. The queen may be suffering from a nutritional deficiency (such as lack of vitamin A), or she may have been mated at the wrong time.	A proper diagnosis of the cause of infertility can only be made after a thorough veterinary examination.
Male infertility	Infertility is very rare in male cats, but it may be due to an infection of the male reproductive organs or an inherited problem. Although a male cat with one undescended testicle (monorchid) can still be fertile, a cat with both testicles undescended (cryptorchid) will probably be sterile.	A proper diagnosis of the cause of infertility can only be made after a thorough veterinary examination. Do not breed from a monorchid cat, since the condition is inherited.
Ovarian cysts	A queen that is not mated may develop ovarian cysts. These cysts produce large quantities of the female sex hormone, which causes frequent or continuous heat periods.	Consult a vet if a queen has abnormal heat cycles.
Abortion and resorption	Miscarriage may be brought on by stress, trauma, an infection, or a fetal abnormality. Signs of miscarriage include bleeding and discharge from the vulva, and the onset of premature labor. Developing kittens less than seven weeks old may sometimes be absorbed from the uterus.	If you notice any unusual signs that may indicate a premature birth, you should contact a vet immediately.
Queening problems	Most cats have no difficulty in giving birth, but occasionally a queen may require assistance *(see pages 174–175)*.	Consult a vet immediately if a cat appears distressed during queening.
Metritis	The uterus can become infected following a difficult birth, particularly if a queen is elderly. Signs may include abdominal pain and a bloody discharge from the vulva.	Consult a vet immediately if there are any abnormal signs following queening.
Pyometra	An accumulation of fluid in the uterus is most common in aging queens. Signs include loss of appetite, high fever, depression, and a vulval discharge.	Consult a vet immediately. An affected cat will need to be spayed.
Mastitis	Mastitis is an inflammation of the mammary glands. The glands appear reddened and swollen, and the kittens are unable to suckle and may show signs of hunger or weakness.	Consult a vet immediately. In severe cases, the kittens may need to be reared by a foster mother or by hand.

FEMALE REPRODUCTIVE PROBLEMS

While a spayed cat will not be affected, an unneutered female cat may suffer from several disorders of the reproductive tract. Pyometra is due to a degeneration of the uterus, occurring as the queen gets older. Cysts develop in the uterus, causing inflammation and the womb to fill up with fluid. The condition can result in toxemia and death if not treated. Immediately after giving birth, a queen may suffer a prolapse of the uterus, in which the womb is pushed outside the body. If this happens, contact a vet immediately, since the condition can lead to severe shock and death. Other health problems associated with the female reproductive system include ovarian cysts, infertility, miscarriage, and problems with queening *(see pages 174-175)*.

Birth problems *(left)*
Seeking veterinary help sooner rather than later is the rule for queening.

NURSING PROBLEMS

Several disorders can prevent a queen from producing milk. Mastitis causes a swelling of the mammary glands. Lactational tetany ("milk fever") results from a fall in the calcium in the blood.

Perfect mother *(above)*
Most queens are excellent mothers and will suckle orphan kittens.

URINARY DISORDERS

Problems that affect a cat's urinary system warrant urgent veterinary investigation, since such disorders can be serious and life-threatening. If your cat strains when passing urine, or cannot pass any at all, you should contact a vet at once. A cat's urine is fairly clear or pale yellow; if it becomes cloudy or colored, this may indicate a bladder infection or even the start of kidney disease. Excessive thirst and frequent urination can sometimes be a sign of diabetes or liver disease, while incontinence may often be associated with a hormonal imbalance or a spinal injury. To prevent urinary problems, make sure water is always available, and do not feed a cat only on dry food, since too little fluid can lead to a urinary obstruction.

Drinking too much
If your cat is drinking to excess or passing more urine than usual it must be examined by a vet without delay, since this may be a sign of kidney disease.

THE URINARY SYSTEM

Urination
The urinary system is responsible for keeping optimum levels of useful chemicals in the blood and eliminating toxic ones. Waste material is filtered through the kidneys and released as urine down the ureters to the bladder. The urine then passes through the urethra and out of the body.

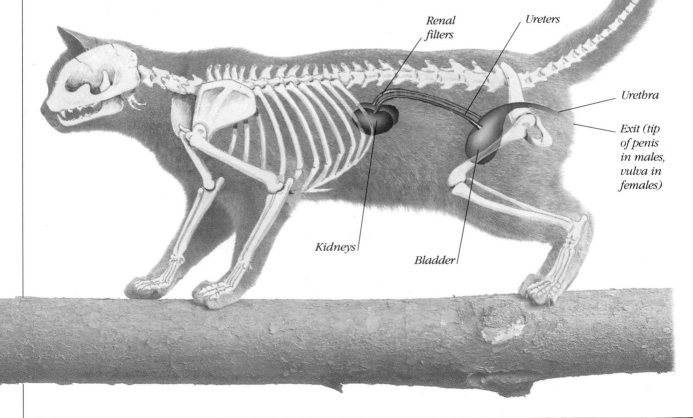

Renal filters

Ureters

Urethra

Exit (tip of penis in males, vulva in females)

Kidneys

Bladder

URINARY DISORDERS

Disorder	Description and signs	Action
Chronic kidney disease	This is the most common disorder that affects elderly cats. The gradual deterioration of the functioning of the kidneys makes it difficult for a cat to eliminate waste products from its body. An affected cat may start to urinate more frequently and will have an increased thirst. Other common signs of kidney disease are weight loss, bad breath, and mouth ulcers.	Consult a vet, who will be able to make a proper diagnosis after taking a sample of blood. Careful dietary management is essential in order to compensate for kidney damage.
Acute kidney disease	Acute kidney disease is not as common as the chronic form and usually affects younger cats. It may be caused by bacterial or viral infection, or as the result of a cat swallowing a toxic substance. The signs are vomiting and loss of appetite, severe depression, and dehydration.	Consult a vet immediately, who will try to combat the toxin if the disease is caused by poisoning. Fluids need to be given to combat dehydration.
Urinary obstruction or Feline Urological Syndrome (FUS)	Minute crystals or a sandy sludge can sometimes cause a blockage of the bladder if they build up to plug the urethra. This particularly affects neutered male cats because the urethra of the female cat is relatively wide. A cat with urinary problems will strain to pass a little bloodstained urine and, in severe cases, it may not be able to pass any urine at all. The bladder may be distended and the abdomen tense and painful to the touch. This condition causes an affected cat a great deal of pain and distress.	Urgent veterinary treatment is required to relieve a bladder obstruction. Left untreated, a cat may die in two days. Careful dietary control is needed to ensure that a cat has a high water intake. A cat should not ingest excessive amounts of magnesium, since this produces an acid urine.
Cystitis	An inflammation of the bladder is most commonly caused by a bacterial infection or may be associated with FUS (see above). In Australia, cystitis can be caused by a bladder worm. Signs include frequent urination accompanied by straining and an increased thirst. The urine may be blood-stained and the cat may persistently lick its rear end.	Consult a vet immediately in order to ensure that the condition does not worsen – if this happens, the bladder may become blocked.
Incontinence	Frequent or constant urination due to a loss of voluntary control may be due to old age, injury, or an infection of the bladder. This is not the same as urine marking or spraying, which is territorial behavior.	If there are any other signs, such as straining, consult a vet immediately. Do not limit the cat's water intake.

URINARY INFECTIONS

An inflammation of the bladder, known as cystitis, may be due to a bacterial infection and can be treated successfully if it is detected early. The symptoms of infection are frequent urination with some discomfort, straining, and constant licking under the tail. Cystitis can affect both sexes, but it is mainly toms and young neutered males that suffer from the more serious Feline Urological Syndrome. If a cat does not drink enough water, or is fed only dry food, the urine may become too concentrated and the salts in it form a sandy deposit or stones, which block the urethra, the narrow passage to the outside.

The cat then experiences difficulty and pain when urinating. FUS is not usually found in females. It is a condition that requires emergency veterinary treatment.

Straining (below)
A cat should show no signs of discomfort when passing urine.

KIDNEY PROBLEMS

The kidneys are often the first organs to show signs of aging, deteriorating gradually (see page 138). Without treatment the cat's condition may worsen, until the kidneys produce little urine, resulting in a buildup of toxic material inside the cat, which can be fatal. Urgent medical treatment is needed before the condition becomes irreversible. However, if the symptoms are recognized early enough, the cat may be treated successfully and go on to enjoy a long and normal life. Apart from deterioration through old age, kidney failure can also occur as the result of an injury, or following a serious disease, such as Feline Infectious Peritonitis (see page 111).

NERVOUS DISORDERS

The grace, coordination, and agility of cats require a highly sophisticated system of nervous control. The intricate network of nerves runs without mishap for most of the time, but if a problem does occur, it tends to be of a serious nature. Although relatively rare, cats are occasionally subject to fits and seizures. These may be due to several causes, including brain tumor, poisoning, or an inherited epileptic condition. However, the most common cause of nervous problems is physical damage as a result of road traffic accidents. An inflammation of the brain or spinal cord can be associated with some infectious diseases. Paralysis of a limb can result if the spinal cord or the nerves supplying that part of the body are damaged in an accident. If the nerves do not heal, the paralysis may be permanent.

Poisoning
If a feline eats a rat or mouse killed with poison, it may become very ill, since the substance often attacks the nervous system.

THE CENTRAL NERVOUS SYSTEM

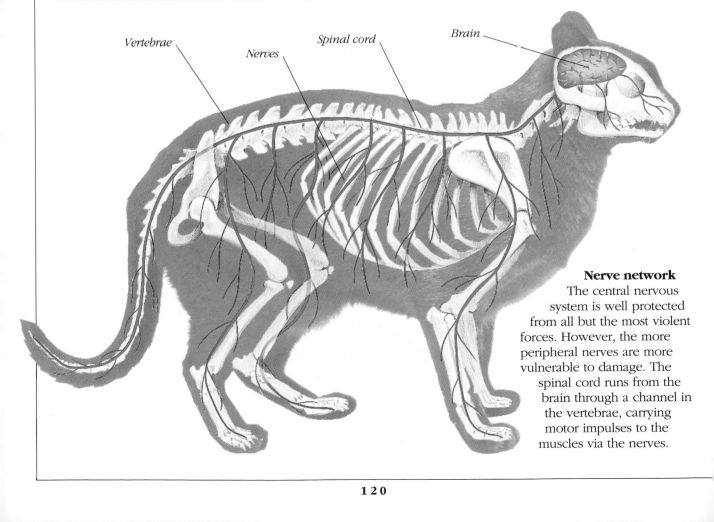

Vertebrae

Nerves

Spinal cord

Brain

Nerve network
The central nervous system is well protected from all but the most violent forces. However, the more peripheral nerves are more vulnerable to damage. The spinal cord runs from the brain through a channel in the vertebrae, carrying motor impulses to the muscles via the nerves.

NERVOUS DISORDERS

Disorder	Description and signs	Action
Brain damage	Severe trauma to the brain is most often due to a road traffic accident or fall and is usually fatal. Strokes are very rare in cats. They are due to a blood clot forming in a vessel to the brain and often result in a loss of functioning of one part of the body. Brain damage can also be caused by a tumor or a congenital defect, or by the spread of a bacterial infection from another part of the body.	Urgent veterinary treament is essential following an accident or fall, especially where head injuries are suspected. Most cats recover from a minor stroke, but they may need treatment for residual problems, such as loss of sight or recurring seizures.
Meningitis	This uncommon nervous disease affects the membrane covering the brain and the spinal cord. It results in fever, dilated pupils, loss of appetite, and convulsions.	Urgent veterinary treatment is required. The vet may take a specimen of the spinal fluid for examination.
Encephalitis	Encephalitis is an inflammation of the brain itself and may be caused by some viruses such as rabies, or bacterial infection. Signs can be variable and include fever, dilated pupils, seizures, and paralysis.	Urgent veterinary treatment is required. The vet will need to establish the cause of the infection.
Seizures	Seizures are relatively rare in cats. They may be connected with brain damage, poisoning, or a vitamin deficiency or may even be inherited. Epileptic episodes may begin when a kitten is about six months old or they may suddenly start following an accident or blow to the head.	Consult a vet immediately. Do not move a convulsing cat. Seizures can sometimes be controlled by anticonvulsant drugs.
Paralysis	The spinal cord and nerves supplying a part of the body may be damaged following an accident, resulting in paralysis of the affected area. This usually happens to a cat's tail or limb. The cat will be unable to bear any weight on the affected limb and may drag it along the ground.	If the nerve is severely damaged and the limb is fractured in an accident, amputation may be necessary. Most cats are able to cope surprisingly well with only three legs.
Feline Dysautonomia (Key-Gaskell Syndrome)	The cause of this rare condition, which affects a cat's nervous system, is unknown. Signs include rapid weight loss, appetite loss, vomiting, regurgitation of food, and pupil dilation.	Urgent veterinary attention is essential if there are to be any prospects of the cat recovering.
Poisoning	There are a number of household substances that are extremely poisonous to a cat should it ingest them. Poisoning may cause signs such as convulsions or muscle tremors.	Seek veterinary attention immediately if you suspect that your cat has been poisoned (see pages 166–167).
Loss of balance	Unsteadiness and lack of coordination when walking may be the result of faulty development, injury, vitamin deficiency, or a disorder of the inner ear (see page 107).	Seek veterinary attention immediately for a thorough examination of the cat.

TESTING REFLEXES

While half the nervous system is concerned with feeling, using the sensory nerves, the other half controls the cat's movement with the motor nerves. Examining a cat's reflexes is the first step in investigating any nervous disorder. A cat's reflexes (see page 159) give an indication of which part of the nervous system is not working normally. A vet may also test the ability of the cat's pupil to contract when a bright light is shone into the eye. A semiconscious cat may be unable to react to stimulus if it is suffering from shock. X-ray examinations and samples of blood or fluid from the spinal cord may also be required if a cat is suffering from any suspected nervous disorder.

If there is no feeling in a limb, or an absence of reflexes, and the cat is unable to control its urine or fecal movements, the prospects for recovery are not very good. However, a cat can recover from some neurological injuries, and an assessment must be carried out by a vet in every case.

Feline Dysautonomia (below)
Permanently dilated pupils are a sign of this rare disease.

BLOOD AND HEART DISORDERS

Disorders of the blood are more prevalent in cats than problems with the heart. Even though the heart is fairly small, it is well adapted to the feline lifestyle, capable of rapidly accelerating from a resting heart rate to one that provides the blood circulation needed for sudden bursts of action. As the heart ages, these periods of activity become less frequent, but it is only when there is advanced deterioration of the heart that the cat gets breathless and reluctant to move at all. Heart disease is not common, but can result from old age or be due to a nutrient deficiency, such as a lack of taurine in the diet, but this only follows gross errors such as feeding a cat exclusively on dog food.

Listening in
Part of any routine examination of a cat's circulatory system includes listening to the heart. A vet can usually assess heart function with a stethoscope, but other, more sophisticated techniques are also available.

THE CIRCULATORY SYSTEM

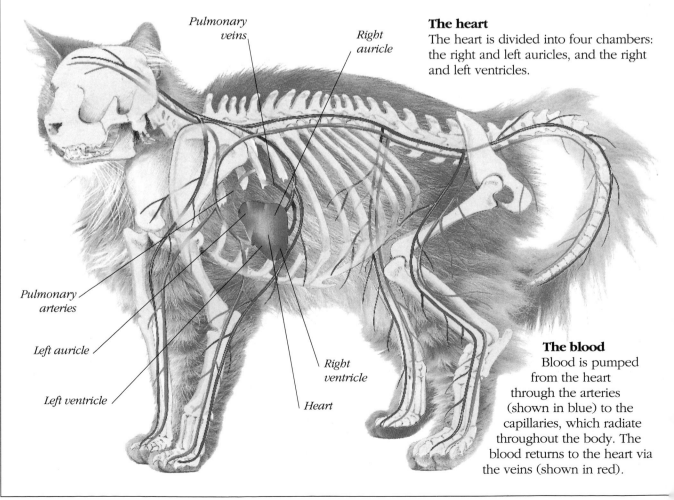

Pulmonary veins

Right auricle

The heart
The heart is divided into four chambers: the right and left auricles, and the right and left ventricles.

Pulmonary arteries

Left auricle

Left ventricle

Right ventricle

Heart

The blood
Blood is pumped from the heart through the arteries (shown in blue) to the capillaries, which radiate throughout the body. The blood returns to the heart via the veins (shown in red).

BLOOD AND HEART DISORDERS

Disorder	Description and signs	Action
Feline Leukemia Virus (FeLV)	FeLV causes cancer of the white blood cells and lymph system. It can only be spread by direct contact with an affected cat and is most common in multicat households. Symptoms of the virus are not very specific but include weight loss, vomiting, diarrhea, labored breathing, and anemia.	There is no effective treatment for FeLV. Blood tests are available to detect the virus. All cats that test positive must be isolated. A vaccine is now available.
Feline Immunodeficiency Virus (FIV)	FIV is similar to the HIV virus that affects humans, but it is specific to cats. The virus suppresses the immune system, making the cat susceptible to infection. It is not transmitted sexually but is spread through the saliva of an infected cat. A cat with FIV may seem slightly ill at first, but it may then develop secondary infections such as anemia (see below).	A blood test is available to diagnose the disease, but there is no treatment or vaccine to combat the FIV virus. Humans cannot catch AIDS from cats.
Anemia	A cat suffering from anemia has a shortage of red blood cells, which reduces the amount of oxygen carried in the blood. Signs of anemia include pallor of the gums, lethargy, weakness, and loss of appetite.	Consult a vet immediately if you notice any signs of anemia. Treatment depends on the cause of the illness.
Feline Infectious Anemia (FIA)	FIA is caused by a small blood parasite that damages red blood cells and causes severe anemia (see above). It is transmitted by bloodsucking parasites such as fleas and ticks.	FIA can be confirmed by a blood test. Treatment involves antibiotics, iron supplements, and blood transfusions.
Heart disease	Kittens may occasionally be born with heart abnormalities – most of them die when they are under one year old. Other problems involve a deterioration of the heart muscle, causing it to become inflamed or damaged (cardiomyopathy). The heart valves may get weaker or become blocked in an elderly cat. Signs of heart disease include heavy breathing, a bluish tinge to the gums, and a tendency to tire easily.	Consult a vet immediately if a cat shows any signs of heart disease. Treatment depends on the heart problem, but drugs can be prescribed for certain conditions.
Thrombosis	This is caused by clotted blood blocking a vessel and cutting off the blood supply. The first sign may be a sudden paralysis of the hind legs, which will feel cold to the touch.	Urgent veterinary treatment is essential. Surgery may sometimes be possible, but the recovery rate is low.
Heartworm	This uncommon feline disease usually occurs only in hot, humid parts of the world. Signs include breathing difficulties, weight loss, and a buildup of fluid in the abdomen.	If detected early, a vet can prescribe drugs to prevent the heartworm larvae from developing into adult worms.

HEARTWORM

In hot, humid countries, the heartworm (Dirofilaria immitis) can infest cats, although it more commonly parasitizes dogs. Preventive drugs are given in high-risk areas, but treatment is difficult, since killing the adult worm can cause fatal blockage of a blood vessel. The microscopic larvae, meanwhile, are often difficult to detect in a cat's blood, since they are not very numerous. However they can be prevented from developing into the harmful adult worms with a course of drug treatment.

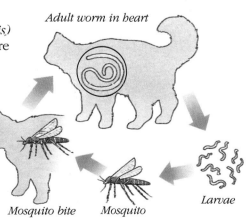

Adult worm in heart

Mosquito bite   *Mosquito*   *Larvae*

Life of a heartworm (above)
The worm's microscopic offspring are transmitted via a mosquito bite and develop in the heart.

BLOOD TESTING

Infectious anemia is due to tiny organisms that can inhabit the red blood cells and destroy them. A vet can identify these parasites by taking a blood sample. Other serious feline blood disorders are cancer of the white blood cells due to Feline Leukemia Virus, and the suppression of a cat's immune system as a result of Feline Immunodeficiency Virus, a relative of the AIDS virus. There are blood tests available for the detection of these different, lethal viruses and isolation procedures to prevent infection spreading. Consult a vet if any of these conditions is likely.

DISEASES TRANSMISSIBLE TO HUMANS

The infectious diseases that can be passed between humans and other animals are called zoonoses. As far as cats are concerned, however, the risk to humans is small, mainly because cats are very clean animals. In addition, infectious microorganisms tend to thrive only in particular species. For example, swine fever only affects pigs, and the common cold is confined to humans. There are a few diseases that can be passed from animals to humans. The most important feline zoonoses include rabies, toxoplasmosis, and skin irritations. However, the risk of catching any disease from your cat is minimal.

Rabies
Rabies can be passed from wild animals to pets, and then to humans.

RABIES WORLDWIDE

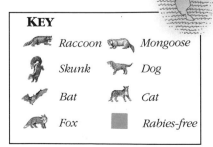

Map of vectors
The map shows the main vectors of rabies in different parts of the world.

KEY

Raccoon		Mongoose	
Skunk		Dog	
Bat		Cat	
Fox		Rabies-free	

VECTORS OF RABIES

The most serious disease that humans can get from animals is rabies. All warm-blooded animals can be victims of rabies, but only a few animals are vectors, or carriers, of the disease. The main vectors are animals such as foxes, wolves, raccoons, skunks, bats, dogs, and mongooses. Only parts of Europe (including Great Britain), Iceland, Japan, Hawaii, the West Indies, Australia, New Zealand, and Antarctica are rabies-free. These countries must take strict quarantine measures to safeguard their status (see page 50).

DISEASES TRANSMISSIBLE TO HUMANS

Disease	Description and signs	Action
Rabies	Rabies is the most dangerous disease that can be passed from animals to humans. It is highly contagious and is transmitted through the saliva of an infected animal. There are three stages to the disease. The first stage is marked by a change in behavior. A normally friendly cat may become nervous and try to hide itself away. The cat may become increasingly aggressive and excited in the second stage, and may try to bite and scratch anyone who approaches it. The final stage is paralysis and coma, which ends in death.	There is no known treatment for rabies once the cat (or human) is showing clinical signs of the disease. Routine preventive vaccination is required by law in some parts of the United States where rabies is present. A cat suspected of having rabies must be isolated, and immediate veterinary treatment should be sought.
Bacterial enteritis	A cat may occasionally eat contaminated or badly cooked meat containing bacteria and suffer from enteritis (inflammation of the intestine). *Salmonella* bacteria are a rare cause of enteritis but can be transmitted to humans. Signs of infection are fever, vomiting and diarrhea, and excessive drinking to replace lost fluids.	Consult a vet if vomiting or diarrhea are severe or persist. The cat may require antibiotics to treat the bacterial infection. Good hygiene is essential, because an affected cat may be a potential human health risk.
Tuberculosis	Tuberculosis can infect cats and other domestic animals as well as man, but it is now uncommon in most countries. The disease is usually transmitted by a cat drinking infected milk, but it can also be passed on by owners to their pets. The lungs and abdomen are the main body systems affected. Signs include fever and severe loss of condition.	Treatment of an infected cat may be possible, but the public health risks have to be considered.
Toxoplasmosis	This common disease is caused by a microscopic intestinal parasite that can infect many species of animal and can be transmitted to humans. A cat becomes infected by eating contaminated prey or raw meat. Most infected cats show no signs of illness, but signs of a severe infection may include fever, loss of appetite, weight loss, and breathing difficulties. Humans may be infected by handling contaminated cat feces or, more likely, from handling infected raw meat.	The disease can be controlled by preventing a cat from scavenging and by cooking meat thoroughly before feeding the cat. Pregnant women are at risk and should avoid handling soiled litter. Blood tests are available to screen those at risk.
Skin problems	Ringworm is a common fungal skin infection *(see page 101)* that is contagious to humans and other animals. It causes small, round, bald patches on a cat's head and ears and circular red patches on a human's arms and legs. Fleas, lice, and fur mites may sometimes bite humans and cause skin reactions, such as itchiness and red blotches.	Prompt veterinary treatment and disinfection of bedding and grooming equipment is advisable if your cat has ringworm. Fleas and other parasites can be controlled by treatment of animals and their environment.

TOXOPLASMOSIS

Cats are sometimes carriers of the microscopic *Toxoplasma* parasite that can also infect humans. A cat is infected by eating contaminated raw meat, and cysts are then shed in the animal's feces. The risks to humans are greatest from handling infected, raw meat. Most infections are harmless, but pregnant women are particularly at risk, since the disease may cause abnormalities in the unborn child. Although cats are very careful about burying their droppings, sensible hygiene precautions should be followed when handling soiled cat litter.

BITES AND SCRATCHES

Few cats are aggressive toward humans without provocation. Many of the bites and scratches humans experience are related to clumsy handling or action that is frightening to the cat *(see pages 40–41)*. A cat's mouth contains bacteria, and a bite can become infected if it is not cleaned and treated with antiseptic. If a cat bite becomes swollen or painful, you should seek medical attention. Cat scratches can also introduce infection, and even fever (known as cat-scratch fever), and should always be washed carefully.

Teeth and claws (*above*)
When provoked, a cat can use its teeth and claws to defend itself.

Chapter 7
NURSING

CATS THAT are sick or injured, and those recovering after a surgical operation, need careful observation, loving support and attention, and a degree of privacy. Try to create a quiet, clean, comfortable area as the feline sick room. Keep a medicine chest well stocked with essential items such as a thermometer, syringe, and dosing gun ready in case of illness. Sick cats may need to be tempted to eat a few nourishing morsels to keep their strength up. You should administer medicines in a gentle but firm way, so that you cause the sick cat the least possible distress. Consult the vet about any special nursing or feeding requirements for your cat's condition.

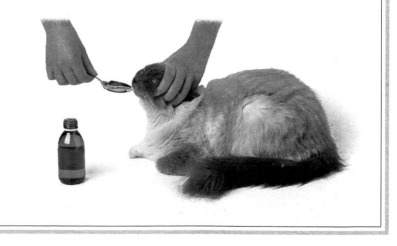

RESTRAINING A CAT

Most cats are not difficult to handle and restrain, but they do have to be taken in their own time with a kindly and gentle approach. Your aim should always be less rather than more restraint. It is unwise for untrained people to attempt to restrain a cat that is not used to being handled; feral cats and most farm cats are particularly resistant to being held. A lively pet may need to be restrained when being examined by a vet.

The methods of firm restraint shown on these pages should only be carried out to control a difficult cat. It is important not to use any unnecessary force, since this will frighten the cat and could even cause it injury. You may find it easiest to wrap an uncooperative cat in a towel when administering medicines at home. It is now possible to buy "masks" and bags to use at home with an unruly cat. Talk calmly and confidently to the cat while it is being examined, in order to reassure it.

HOLDING A CAT FOR EXAMINATION

Examining the head
A veterinary technician restrains the cat by holding its fore legs gently but firmly. Her forearms hold down the cat's body, allowing the vet to examine its head.

Examining the body
A calm cat is easily restrained by holding the shoulders while the skin and coat are examined by the vet.

RESTRAINING A DIFFICULT CAT

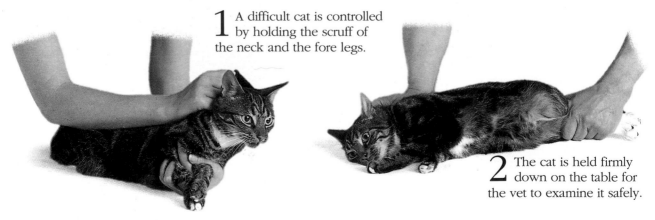

1 A difficult cat is controlled by holding the scruff of the neck and the fore legs.

2 The cat is held firmly down on the table for the vet to examine it safely.

WRAPPING A CAT IN A TOWEL

1 When maximum restraint is needed, a large, thick towel is useful. The cat is held firmly on the towel by the scruff. It is best not to let the cat see the towel beforehand.

Hold the cat firmly on the towel

The paws must be wrapped in the towel

3 A towel wrapped firmly around the cat prevents the cat from scratching when being treated or examined.

2 The cat is wrapped quickly in the towel, keeping hold of the scruff all the time.

SCRUFFING A CAT

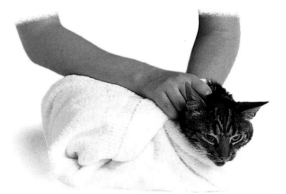

Scruffing may help control a difficult cat

Clothespins
One or two broad-ended clothespins placed on the scruff of the neck can immobilize a cat in the same way as lifting it up by the scruff.

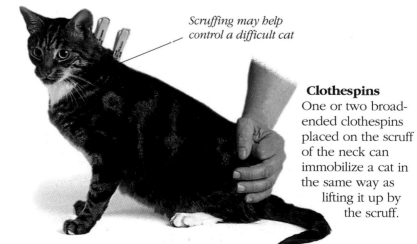

HANDLE WITH CARE

Do not attempt to restrain an angry or frightened cat by holding it by the scruff or by using the "clothespin" method unless you are experienced in handling cats. You should never prolong any restraint if it is causing the animal distress. This applies to all methods of handling and restraint.

ADMINISTERING MEDICINE

You may be given some tablets or medication to administer at home after visiting the vet. Getting your cat to take the medicine it needs but does not want requires a gentle but firm approach. It is best if the cat is placed on a table or other raised surface; some cats will need to be restrained by an assistant. If the cat tries to scratch or bite, it should be wrapped in a towel *(see page 129)*. You should not try to hide medicine in food since a cat can usually detect any additions to its food bowl by smell and may refuse to eat.

GIVING A TABLET

Hold the cat's head from above

1 While an assistant holds the cat, gently enclose its head with your fingers. Do not ruffle its whiskers.

2 Grasp the head between forefinger and thumb and tip it back. Press lightly on the jaw to open the cat's mouth.

3 Place the tablet as far back as possible on the tongue at the back of the cat's mouth.

4 Close the cat's mouth and gently stroke the throat to encourage it to swallow the tablet.

GIVING A TABLET ON YOUR OWN

1 If your cat is gentle and docile, you can give it a tablet without any assistance. Grasp the cat's head with one hand and open its mouth with the other.

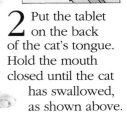

Tablet

2 Put the tablet on the back of the cat's tongue. Hold the mouth closed until the cat has swallowed, as shown above.

GIVING A TABLET USING A DOSING GUN

*Fire the tablet
into the cat's
mouth*

1 An alternative method of giving a tablet is to use a pill or dosing gun, which you can obtain from your vet.

2 Open the cat's mouth as shown opposite and fire the tablet with a little water to the back of the throat. Hold the mouth closed until the cat has swallowed.

GIVING MEDICINE WITH A SYRINGE

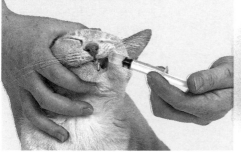

Using a plastic syringe, slowly squirt the liquid into the cat's mouth. Administer the medicine slowly so that it does not go down the wrong way.

GIVING AN INJECTION

An injection is the most effective way of administering medicine to a cat, and this is almost always done by a vet. However, when injections are required every day, for instance in the treatment of diseases such as feline diabetes, you may have to carry out this procedure yourself. Your vet will supply you with sterile syringes and discuss the procedure with you.

*Draw the medicine
into the syringe*

1 Hold the cat firmly and make a little "tent" of loose skin at the scruff of the neck.

2 Insert the needle under the skin at the cat's neck, and slowly inject the medication.

TREATING EYES AND EARS

There are several feline eye and ear conditions that require treatment with drops or ointment prescribed by a vet. After consulting your vet you will probably be given a course of medicines to administer at home. (Never try to treat your cat with medicines intended for humans or without getting proper advice.) Your vet will be happy to demonstrate the best way to apply medication to the eyes and ears.

You should administer eye and ear drops quickly and carefully, using the minimum amount of restraint *(see pages 128–129)*. Follow the directions given by the vet and, even if the problem appears to clear up, continue the course of treatment for as long as advised to ensure that the condition does not recur.

APPLYING EYE OINTMENT

1 Hold the cat's head still with one hand. Using the other hand, gently squeeze a line of ointment onto the eyeball. Do not let the tube touch the eye.

2 Close the eyelids and hold closed for a few seconds to allow the ointment to spread over the eye.

APPLYING EYE DROPS

1 Gently clean the area around the eyes, wiping away any discharge from the corners of the eyes with a dampened cotton ball.

2 Holding the cat's head firmly with one hand, apply the required number of eye drops in both eyes.

3 Allow the eyes to bathe in the drops for a few seconds. Gently hold the eyes closed as above.

ADMINISTERING EAR DROPS

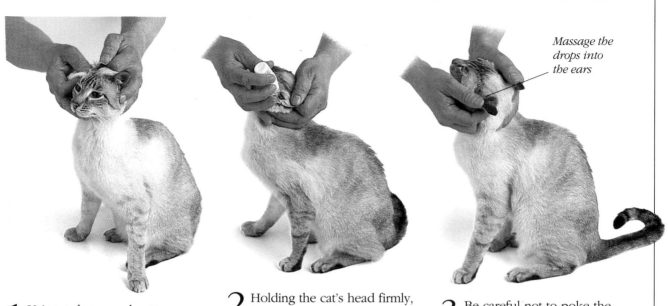

Massage the drops into the ears

1 Using a dampened cotton ball, wipe away any dirt from the inside of the ear.

2 Holding the cat's head firmly, fold the outer ear back and administer the required number of drops in both ears.

3 Be careful not to poke the dropper into the cat's ears. Gently massage the ears.

INHERITED EYE AND EAR PROBLEMS

Deaf white cat
Deafness can be associated with the gene that gives a white cat its coat color. It causes a degeneration of the inner ear.

Longhaired cat
Some pedigree longhaired cats are very prone to blocked tear ducts, which result in runny eyes.

Siamese cat
Some Siamese cats suffer from reduced binocular vision or double vision, for which they compensate by squinting. Careful breeding has reduced the number of cats affected.

Abyssinian cat (right)
Certain breeds, such as Abyssinian and Siamese cats, are prone to inherited eye problems.

SURGERY AND AFTERCARE

Most cats will need to undergo surgery under a general anesthetic at some point in their lives. Although modern techniques of surgery have reduced the dangers to a minimum, there is still a small risk involved with any type of operation. A cat makes a good surgical patient; it adapts well to cage rest and it recovers quickly after major operations.

After an operation, a cat needs to be kept warm and quiet, and its behavior should be closely observed. If the cat is restless or has a fractured limb, it may have to be confined to a pen. A cat recovering from an illness may need to be kept indoors.

Convalescence
A cat must be kept quiet and carefully watched for a week or two after an operation. Try to keep it confined to one room and prevent it from biting its stitches or removing its dressing.

SURGICAL OPERATIONS

The operating theater
Veterinary surgery requires similar sterility precautions to human operations.

PRE-OPERATIVE CARE

If your cat is to undergo a routine operation, such as neutering or teeth scaling, arrange for it to be done when you have some time to care for your pet. The cat will not be allowed to eat or drink for 12 hours prior to the operation. This may seem hard, but it is important because it reduces the risk of the cat vomiting while under the anesthetic. When you deliver your cat to the clinic or hospital, you can ask when you can telephone to find out about its progress. A cat will usually be allowed to go home the same day.

ANIMAL HOSPITALS

At the animal hospital or veterinary clinic, the cat will be kept in a cage under regular supervision until it has recovered from the anesthetic. When it wakes it will be unsteady on its feet for several hours. You will be allowed to take the cat home only when the vet is satisfied that it is on the mend. The cat may be kept at the veterinary clinic for two or three days for observation following a serious operation.

Cage rest
A cat is usually put in a recovery cage after a surgical operation to allow for close observation and undisturbed rest. Some hospitals have television monitors to help watch over the animals after surgery.

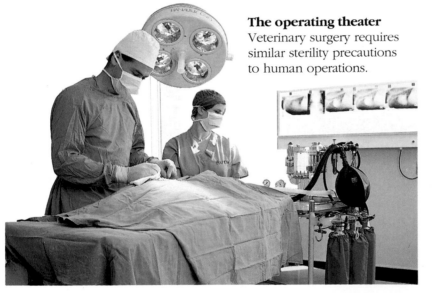

POST-OPERATIVE CARE

Bandages

If a cat has a dressing covering a wound, it may do its utmost to remove it. Cover it with an elastic bandage to keep it in place for as long as possible. Keep a cat confined as directed.

RECOVERY TIMES

Most cats recover from surgical operations very quickly. Stitches may either dissolve within 7–10 days or may need to be removed by the vet. Before surgery, the fur around the site of the operation will have been shaved; this will take several weeks to grow back.

General nursing

A cat recovering from an operation must be kept warm and quiet. Make the cat comfortable by wrapping it in a large towel or blanket or by putting it in a cardboard box.

Elizabethan collar

A cat should be prevented from pulling out its stitches. An Elizabethan collar, fitted by a vet, is a simple solution that will prevent a cat from worrying a wound. Consult a vet if you notice any swelling or discharge from the wound site.

Veterinary care

If you notice any change in your cat's condition after an operation, report it immediately to a vet.

ALTERNATIVE MEDICINE

There is a growing interest and awareness in alternatives to established conventional medicine for treating cats and dogs. While homeopathic and herbal approaches can be used to treat certain ailments, you still need to consult a vet to get a proper diagnosis. Some vets even specialize in alternative medicine and can prescribe a suitable treatment for your cat. Alternative medicine cannot cure serious conditions that require surgery, but it can be used to treat many minor disorders and prevent them from recurring. For example, homeopathic creams can be used to help various common feline skin complaints.

Garlic

Garlic is reputed to act as a flea repellent and may increase a cat's resistance to infections.

NURSING A SICK CAT

A sick cat that is recovering from an operation, or that needs to be nursed at home through an illness, requires special care. For the best results, it should be cared for in familiar surroundings by people it knows and trusts. Try to make your sick cat comfortable by keeping it clean, warm, and dry. Your vet will give you instructions if your cat requires a special diet.

KEEPING WARM

The sick room
To make a sick bed for your invalid pet, cut a hole in one side of a large cardboard box. Line it with newspapers, a towel, and a lukewarm hot water bottle. The box should be placed in a quiet corner.

FEEDING A SICK CAT

Loss of appetite
A sick cat often needs to be coaxed to eat. Feed small, frequent meals, warmed to blood heat.

Spoonfeeding
If a cat refuses to eat or drink, try feeding it liquids with a spoon. Allow the cat to swallow after every few drops.

Spoonfeeding medicine
A calm cat can be spoonfed liquid medicines. This can be messy, but try to get as much of the medicine as possible into the cat's mouth.

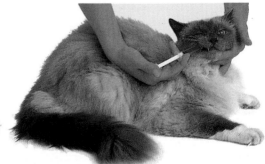

Forcefeeding
A weak cat can be fed small amounts of liquid food with a dropper or a syringe *(see page 131)*.

GROOMING A SICK CAT

1 Clear any discharge from around the cat's eyes with a cotton ball dampened in clean, warm water. You can apply a little petroleum jelly to any sore places, but do not put it too near the cat's eyes.

2 Gently wipe away any nasal discharge and crusting around the cat's nostrils. The cat will be able to breathe more easily and will feel better with some of its sense of smell restored.

SAFE DISINFECTANTS

Disinfectants containing phenol are poisonous. Use hydrogen peroxide or a profesionally prepared product to clean the sick room.

Gently wipe the cat's mouth

3 Clean up any saliva or vomit from around the cat's mouth. Clean up the cat's behind if there is any diarrhea, and change the bedding if it becomes soiled.

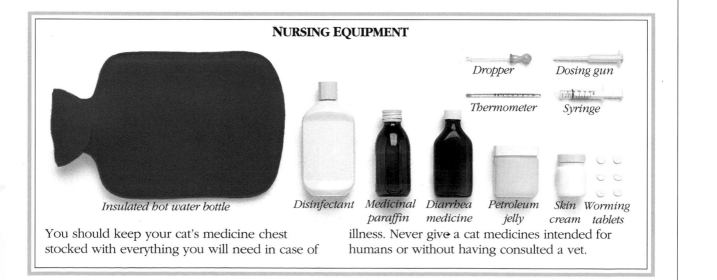

NURSING EQUIPMENT

Dropper

Dosing gun

Thermometer

Syringe

Insulated hot water bottle

Disinfectant

Medicinal paraffin

Diarrhea medicine

Petroleum jelly

Skin cream

Worming tablets

You should keep your cat's medicine chest stocked with everything you will need in case of illness. Never give a cat medicines intended for humans or without having consulted a vet.

CARING FOR AN ELDERLY CAT

Old age is not a specific disease; it comes to us all. As a cat gets older, the vital organs of its body deteriorate at different rates. Changes in the heart, brain, kidneys, and liver are the most life-threatening. Fortunately, these major organs have reasonable reserves of functional activity; more than half of the kidney function may, for example, be lost without the cat showing any signs of illness. Given plenty of loving care and close veterinary management, many cats with quite advanced kidney failure may lead fairly normal, active lives.

Regular health checkups by a vet can improve the quality of life of an elderly cat. An older cat will generally become less active and spend more time sleeping. Try not to disturb its daily routine and ensure that it has a warm bed that is kept in a cozy spot out of drafts.

SIGNS OF OLD AGE

Hearing may become less acute

Eyesight may deteriorate

The coat may become less thick and lose condition

Health checks
You should keep a careful check on the health of an elderly cat. Watch out for any signs of abnormal behavior and examine its eyes, ears, mouth, and coat regularly. Pay particular attention to its mouth and, if your cat will allow it, brush its teeth once a week.

The joints and muscles may become stiff and less supple

The claws may need regular trimming if the cat is inactive

FELINE LIFE SPANS

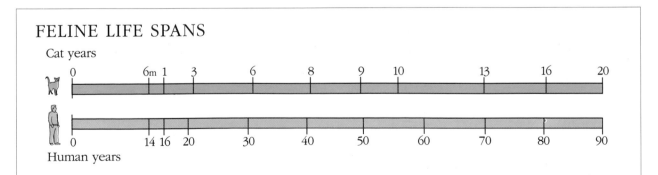

Cat years

| 0 | 6m 1 | 3 | 6 | 8 | 9 | 10 | 13 | 16 | 20 |

Human years

| 0 | 14 16 20 | 30 | 40 | 50 | 60 | 70 | 80 | 90 |

Many people believe that cats age about seven years for every human one. In fact, their development accelerates in the early years and slows down in middle age, as shown in the life span chart above. After the age of ten, signs of old age begin to appear and the time scale is more like ours. Cats over 20 years of age can be looked upon as feline centenarians.

SPECIAL CARE

Feeding
Some cats need less food and fewer calories as they age; others may need more due to poor absorption and digestion *(see page 61)*.

Constipation
Elderly cats may become constipated. Ask your vet about a commercial feline laxative in order to relieve painful constipation.

Weighing
If your cat loses weight while continuing to eat substantial amounts, consult your vet. On the other hand, an older cat that becomes much less active but continues to eat the same amounts of food may become obese.

Veterinary checkups
Regular checkups become more necessary as your cat starts to show the signs of age. They should be carried out at least every three or four months, or whenever your vet advises.

EUTHANASIA
There may come a time when your cat's life needs to be brought to a peaceful end. Any cat that has an untreatable condition, which is causing it pain or distress, can have its life ended gently and with dignity. Vets usually inject an overdose of an anesthetic into a vein, putting the cat into a deep sleep to a point where the animal will not regain consciousness. Your vet will be able to advise you and help you make the difficult decision if your pet is very sick. You may wish to plant a small rose bush or tree, or make a donation to an animal charity to perpetuate the best memories of your pet.

Pet cemeteries
You can bury your cat in a special pet cemetery.

Chapter 8
BREEDING

THE WORLD would certainly be a better place for cats if only wanted kittens were born. Consider carefully the responsibilities of breeding your cat and decide whether or not neutering is the best course of action. Unless you are active in showing your cat and helping to improve the breed, you should not breed it.

You can show your cat even if it is neutered.

Remember that kittens are demanding and need to be found caring homes. If you decide to breed your cat, advance planning is the best way to avoid problems.

HEREDITY AND BREEDING

Every cat inherits certain physical characteristics from both its parents. These characteristics are determined by genes. They represent a set of instructions that determine the cat's coat color, the length of its coat, and the color of its eyes. For every kitten in a litter, the genes are arranged in a different order, so each individual is genetically unique, no matter how similar it is in appearance.

If you wish to breed a show cat, look for a tomcat with suitable characteristics with which to mate your female.

Mother and kitten
This little kitten has a different coat color from both its parents.

A CAT FAMILY TREE

Determining coat color
Kittens with very different coat colors result from the mating of Chocolate and Blue Burmese cats. One of the kittens is the same color as the mother and one is identical to the father, but four have lighter coats. This is because the male is carrying a gene that dilutes the coat color from a silver-gray (Blue) to a lavender-gray (Lilac).

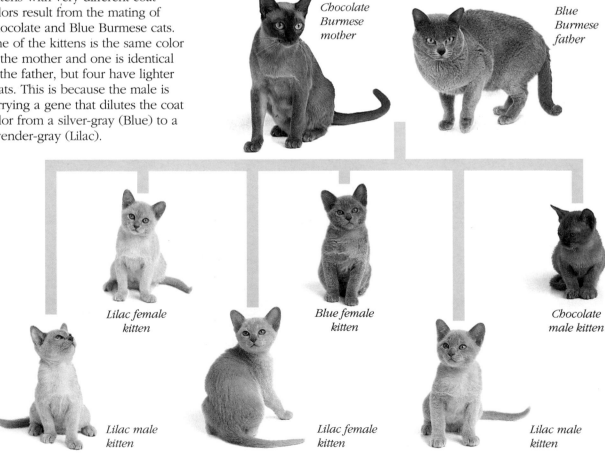

Chocolate Burmese mother

Blue Burmese father

Lilac female kitten

Blue female kitten

Chocolate male kitten

Lilac male kitten

Lilac female kitten

Lilac male kitten

INHERITED CHARACTERISTICS

*A "Stumpy"
Manx has a
residual tail*

Manx cat (left)
The Manx cat is a
very old breed, but if
someone applied today
for its official recognition,
this would probably not
be granted. The Manx
carries a gene that causes
the deformity of taillessness,
which is deadly if it is passed
on by both parents. The mating
of two Manx cats usually results
in the kittens dying before or
shortly after birth.

Rex cat (right)
Despite their similar
appearances, there
are two distinct
breeds of curly coated
Rex cat, namely the
Devon and the Cornish Rex.
Both breeds are believed to
have developed from
separate mutations.

Tortoiseshell cat (above)
The orange gene that results in a
tortoiseshell coat is linked to the
gene that determines the cat's
sex. This means that nearly all
tortoiseshell cats are female. The
very rare male tortoiseshell is
usually sterile.

Rogue genes (left)
A few genes that are passed on from
parents to offspring cause deformities.
While some inherited traits, such as a
kitten being born with extra toes
(polydactyly), are relatively
harmless, others, such as
heart defects, are fatal.

Siamese cat
The Siamese is really
a black cat with its coat
color diluted by an albino-
type gene. This is what gives
a Siamese cat its unique, pale-
colored coat with darker
markings on the head, paws,
and tail. Selective breeding has
intensified the coat color, so
that the body is darkest in
the Seal-point Siamese.

PLANNING A LITTER

Breeding your cat is an important decision that must be considered carefully. A female cat is sexually mature from about six months old and a male cat from about ten months. A queen comes into heat in two-week cycles, and each estrus lasts for two to four days. Even if you take proper precautions, an unneutered queen is almost certain to be mated. It is very difficult to confine a female cat in heat, since she will become restless and "call" or howl, attracting every local tom.

CHOOSING A SUITABLE MATE

The stud cat
If you plan to breed from your pedigree queen, you will need to find a suitable stud cat. Make inquiries at local cat shows or through the relevant breed club, which will be able to supply you with a list of reputable breeders.

COURTSHIP AND MATING

The queen may be hostile to the tom at first

1 The queen is taken to the breeder's stud cat when she comes into heat and starts to "call."

MATING A CAT

- Choose a reputable breeder.
- Cats must be vaccinated and free of STD.
- Never mate a cat that is not perfectly fit and healthy.
- Keep your cat indoors after she returns from the stud.

---

2 When the female begins to show an interest in the tom, the two cats are put together in the same pen. Clip both cats' claws beforehand to prevent injuries in case there is a fight.

The queen sniffs the tom

3 The queen signals that she is ready for mating by rolling provocatively to attract the tom's attention.

The neck-bite immobilizes the queen

4 As part of the courtship ritual, the female rejects the first advance. The tom retreats but renews his overtures a few moments later.

5 The queen raises her rear and makes a "paddling" movement with her hind legs. As the tom mounts, he grasps her by the scruff.

6 The tom penetrates the queen and ejaculates immediately. The female cat may call out at the moment of penetration. Ovulation is stimulated by the act of mating.

Post-coital behavior
After mating, both cats separate and groom themselves. The whole mating sequence will need to be repeated several times over a period of two to three days to ensure that the queen is pregnant.

PREGNANCY AND PRE-NATAL CARE

I f a mating is successsful, the queen will not come into heat as usual two or three weeks later. A pregnant cat shows the first signs of her condition soon after this. Her teats become redder and the surrounding fur may recede slightly. At around three to four weeks, a vet can confirm the pregnancy by gently palpating the cat's abdomen. A healthy cat does not require any special care other than being fed a well-balanced diet. The queen's appetite will increase, and she will gradually put on weight.

SIGNS OF PREGNANCY

The queen will put on about 2–4 lb (1–2 kg)

A pregnant queen
A cat is noticeably fatter after the sixth week of pregnancy. Her abdomen becomes rounded and the teats redden and become very prominent.

The teats are prominent

The abdomen is distended

CARING FOR A PREGNANT CAT

Feeding
A pregnant cat must be fed a nourishing, well-balanced diet, and your vet may also recommend additional feeding during the last weeks. The number of meals should be gradually increased from about the fifth week of pregnancy *(see page 61)*. Consult your vet about dosing your pregnant cat with worming tablets.

Queening box *(above)*
Provide the queen with a warm and comfortable place to give birth. Make a queening box out of a cardboard box, cut down at one side and lined with newspaper.

Active pregnancy
A healthy cat will remain lively throughout the pregnancy. She can be allowed to play with other cats and to jump, and climb, although she may slow down these activities.

A pregnant cat is still interested in playing games

DEVELOPMENT OF THE FETUS

Length of pregnancy
The average length of pregnancy is 65 days, or about nine weeks from the date of the mating. An ultrasound scan can be used six weeks into the pregnancy.

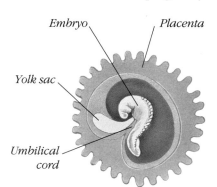

Embryo *Placenta*
Yolk sac
Umbilical cord

2 At 22 days the embryo's head, eyes, and limbs are developing.

3 At 28 days the fetus is about 1 in (2.5 cm) long and all its internal organs have developed.

4 Between 40–45 days the bones of the skeleton form.

1 At 18 days the embryo is still attached to the yolk sac, which provides it with nutrients.

5 The fetus develops rapidly during the last three weeks before the birth. Kittens born earlier than 58 days do not usually survive. Kittens born later than 70 days are likely to be bigger than normal.

QUEENING EQUIPMENT
Prepare for the kittens' birth by making a queening box and having some essential items to hand. This equipment may be needed if you (or the vet) have to assist with the delivery *(see pages 174–175)*. A thermometer may record a drop in the cat's temperature (about 2°F/1°C) a few hours before kittening.

Cotton ball

Petroleum jelly *Safe disinfectant* *Alcohol* *Scissors* *Thermometer*

QUEENING

Keep a careful watch on the queen during the last week of the pregnancy. Make sure that she is accustomed to the queening box and do not allow her to wander off or to hide herself away. The queen's behavior will warn you when the birth is imminent. She may refuse food or vomit before the labor begins. Many kittens are born at night.

GIVING BIRTH

1 The queen starts to breathe heavily, pant, or purr, but not in pain. A clear vaginal discharge may be seen. This first stage of labor can last as long as six hours but is usually shorter.

2 The second stage of labor begins when the queen starts "bearing down." Make a note of the time that she starts to strain, and if a kitten is not born within 30 minutes, contact a vet.

The membrane around the kitten can just be seen

3 In an ideal birth, a kitten enclosed in a bubble-like membrane will appear 15–30 minutes later. Most kittens are born headfirst, but some may be born hind legs first.

4 As soon as a kitten is born, the queen licks it to remove the membrane surrounding it and to stimulate its breathing. The third stage of labor is marked by the expulsion of the afterbirth, which the queen may eat.

HELPING AT THE BIRTH

An inexperienced mother cat may require assistance with the queening. If a queen ignores a newborn kitten or a kitten is only partially delivered, you need to take emergency action immediately or the kitten may die *(see pages 174–175)*. Make sure that your vet is on standby when the kittens are due.

5 Usually, the mother cat instinctively knows what to do. She bites through the umbilical cord with her teeth.

WHEN TO CALL THE VET

Most cats do not need any help with queening. Keep interference to a minimum. Contact a vet if the cat is distressed (*see page 174*).

6 Allow the mother cat to lick the kittens immediately. The queen may take a short rest after one or two kittens have been born and resume her straining a few moments later.

A newborn kitten looks for a teat

7 The newborn kittens may need a little help in finding a teat on which to feed. Make sure that the kittens are placed near their mother's abdomen, and encourage them to suckle as soon as possible.

8 An average litter numbers between two and six kittens and the labor may last for several hours. If the queen shows signs of weariness, she can be revived with a little milk or some of her favorite food.

Happy families

Once the queening is complete, leave the mother and kittens to rest. Make sure that the queen is provided with water, food, and a litter box. She may be reluctant to leave her kittens.

POST-NATAL CARE

Newborn kittens are totally dependent on the mother cat. The cat family should be kept in the queening box, in a warm place. Keep a watch on the kittens, particularly if the queen is inexperienced. As long as the mother is healthy, she will do all that is necessary. The queen will require at least three times more food than usual *(see page 61)*.

MATERNAL CARE

Each kitten has its own preferred teat

Bonding
Shortly after a kitten is born, the mother cat will gently guide it to a teat, and it will start to suckle. The milk produced by the mother cat in the first few days after queening is called "colostrum" and is packed with nutrients and antibodies that will protect the kittens from infection.

The mother cat washes her kittens frequently

Washing
Once the kittens have finished suckling, the mother cat will wash them all over. The queen licks the kittens' bottoms to stimulate excretion of waste products. She will do this until the kittens start to eat solid food.

Suckling
By kneading its mother's body with its paws, a kitten stimulates the flow of milk. If the kittens are restless and cry a lot, this may be a sign that the queen is not producing enough milk. Consult the vet if you suspect that the kittens are not getting enough milk.

Keeping watch

The mother cat carefully guards her litter and dislikes leaving the kittens too often. If any of the kittens strays from the nest, she retrieves it by carrying it by the scruff of the neck. Do not let children pick up or handle the kittens without supervision. Try not to disturb the mother and offspring any more than is necessary.

A straying kitten is closely watched by its mother

FOSTERING KITTENS

The mother cat will not notice one or two extra mouths to feed

Foster mothers

If the mother cat has died, rejected her litter, or cannot produce milk, you will need to find a foster mother. A new queen with a small litter of her own will accept one or two orphan kittens.

Foster care

If you are raising an orphan by bottle you will need to provide the socialization it would have received from its mother and littermates.

ARTIFICIAL FEEDING

Bottle feeding

It is possible to rear orphan kittens by hand. Start by feeding the kittens every two hours with a cat milk replacer. The kittens must also be kept clean and warm. Ask your vet for guidance.

FEEDING EQUIPMENT

Feeding bottle   *Dropper*   *Syringe*

All feeding equipment must be sterilized and the milk made up according to the directions.

EARLY KITTEN CARE

For the first few weeks of their lives, kittens are at their most helpless and need a lot of attention. Up to the age of about three weeks, the mother cat will provide for their physical needs, but you will need to handle and socialize them. The kittens should gradually be weaned off their mother's milk and introduced to solid food. By the age of ten to twelve weeks, the kittens should be fully weaned and ready to leave their mother.

RAISING KITTENS

One day old
A newborn kitten is completely dependent on its mother. Its eyelids are closed and its ears are folded back, so it cannot see or hear.

The kittens instinctively huddle together to keep warm

Three weeks old
Two weeks later, the kittens are fully mobile and eager to explore. They are now ready to be given a little solid food *(see opposite)*.

One week old
The kittens' eyes open at about seven days old. The litter is still very vulnerable and helpless without the mother cat, and the young sleep huddled together for security and warmth.

Four weeks old
Once the kittens are eating solids, they can be trained to use a litter box. Place the box in a quiet spot and put the kittens on it after each feed. Never rub a kitten's nose in any accidental mess that it makes.

Five weeks old

Feed the kittens a range of different foods to encourage good eating habits in later life. Finely minced cooked meat and poached white fish can be given to add a little variety to the diet as an alternative to canned kitten food.

Six weeks old

The kittens learn how to hunt by pouncing on toy prey. Boisterous games with littermates allow them to try out offensive and defensive roles.

Seven weeks old

Regular weighing and monitoring of the kittens' weights *(see page 58)* allows you to keep an eye on their development – however, you may have a problem getting them to sit still on the scales.

Nine weeks old

At eight to nine weeks of age, the kittens should be vaccinated against Feline respiratory disease and Feline Infectious Enteritis. A kitten should not go outside until it has been vaccinated.

WEANING KITTENS		
Age	**Type of food**	**Number of feeds**
3 weeks old	Powdered cat milk substitute, a little finely chopped, cooked meat or kitten food, and mother's milk.	Place in a saucer and give 4–6 times daily.
4 weeks old	Powdered cat milk substitute, finely chopped, cooked meat or kitten food, and mother's milk.	Place in a saucer and give 4–6 times daily.
5 weeks old	Finely chopped, cooked meat or kitten food as well as mother's milk.	Provide solid food 4–5 times daily.
6–8 weeks old	Increase the amount of solid food given and decrease the kittens' access to mother cat's milk.	Provide solid food 3–4 times daily.
8 weeks and older	The kittens are fully weaned. Special kitten foods are needed until they are six months old.	Provide solid food 3–4 times daily.

PREVENTING PREGNANCY

Unless you are the owner of a pedigree cat that you intend to show or breed, you should consider having it neutered to prevent unwanted kittens. Neutering is a routine operation and is normally carried out when a kitten is between four and six months old. Neutering prevents the production of the hormones that govern a cat's sex drive and the development of undesirable behavior. An unneutered tomcat marks its territory by spraying it with pungent urine. An unspayed queen comes into heat every few weeks, when she "calls" to attract males in the vicinity.

Double pregnancy
Two pregnant cats mean double the care when the kittens arrive.

MALE CATS

A castrated cat
A neutered male cat makes a very affectionate and loving pet that is less likely to stray from home or to get into fights than a tomcat.

The head, neck, and shoulders are less muscular than in an intact cat

A tomcat (below)
A tomcat is dominated by its sex drive. The secondary sexual characteristics of a tom are unpleasant for humans and make it a difficult pet to keep indoors. It marks its territory by spraying it with pungent urine.

NEUTERING CHECKLIST

• A cat can be castrated or spayed at any age, provided that it is healthy.
• Early castration prevents a male cat from developing undesirable behavior.
• Alternative methods of birth control are available to prevent a queen from coming into heat.

FEMALE CATS

A spayed cat
A spayed cat looks the same as an unspayed female. Contrary to popular belief, there are no benefits in letting your cat have one litter of kittens before being spayed.

A queen in heat attracts toms by her scent

Sexual behavior (above)
A queen in heat is restless and noisy. If she is confined indoors, she will become frustrated and do her utmost to escape.

A spayed cat looks the same as a queen

The queen (right)
The process of giving birth and raising young will take its toll on a female cat and may cause premature aging. It is cruel to allow a cat to go through the rigors of queening, only to have the unwanted kittens destroyed.

THE NEUTERING OPERATIONS

Castration
A male cat should ideally be neutered at about six months old. Castration is a routine operation and involves the removal of the cat's testes under a general anesthetic. There are normally no stitches. A healthy cat will be back to normal a day after the operation.

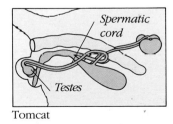

Spermatic cord

Testes

Tomcat

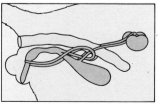

Neutered male

Spaying
A female cat should ideally be neutered at around four or five months old. A queen cannot be neutered while in heat. The operation involves the removal of the cat's uterus and ovaries under a general anesthetic. There will be a small wound on the cat's flank.

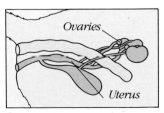

Ovaries

Uterus

Queen

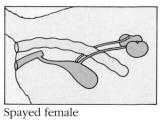

Spayed female

Chapter 9

FIRST AID

LEARN HOW to handle the most common emergencies. Prompt action in such cases as poisoning, choking, drowning, burns, bites, and stings can save life and prevent unnecessary suffering. First aid does not mean setting up a do-it-yourself veterinary practice. Your primary objectives must be to prevent

further injury to the cat, to alleviate pain and distress, and to help begin the recovery process. Getting help from a vet is the highest priority. You should restrict yourself to taking only immediate necessary action to stabilize the cat's condition until veterinary assistance is available.

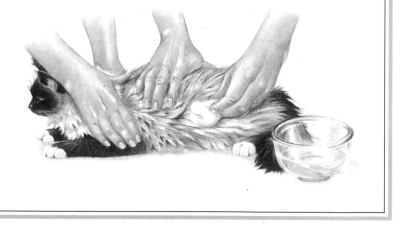

PRINCIPLES OF FIRST AID

First aid is important as an interim measure before professional veterinary help is available, and it may save your cat's life in an emergency. An injured cat may require urgent first aid to stop bleeding, treat shock, and restart or clear its breathing. The objectives of first aid should be: to prevent the cat's condition from worsening; to remove any source of harm; to alleviate pain and suffering; and to help with the recovery process. The absolute rule is to do no harm. Take essential action only and seek advice on the next course of action from a vet as soon as possible.

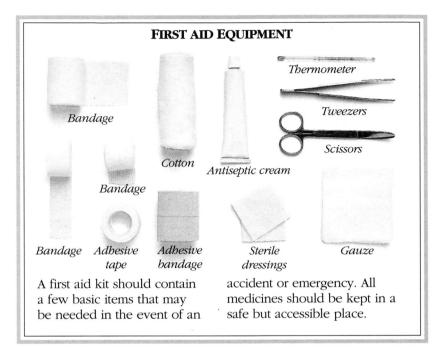

FIRST AID EQUIPMENT

Bandage

Thermometer

Tweezers

Cotton

Scissors

Antiseptic cream

Bandage

Bandage *Adhesive tape* *Adhesive bandage* *Sterile dressings* *Gauze*

A first aid kit should contain a few basic items that may be needed in the event of an accident or emergency. All medicines should be kept in a safe but accessible place.

ASSESSING AN INJURED CAT

1 Open the cat's mouth and pull the tongue forward. Clear the mouth of mucus using a piece of cotton. The head should be tilted downward so that no fluids are inhaled.

2 Count the number of breaths in or out (but not both) for one or two minutes. The rate should be 20–30 breaths per minute.

3 Feel the cat's pulse on the inside of the hind leg. Count the number of beats per minute. The rate should be 160–240 beats per minute. The heartbeat can be felt behind the cat's elbow.

Feeling the pulse

Feeling the heartbeat

CHECKING REFLEXES

Eyelid reflex
You can check the eyelid reflex by gently touching the corner of the cat's eyelid. Do not touch the eyeball itself. A cat should automatically blink if it is at all conscious.

Foot reflex
Gently pinch the web of skin between the toes. A cat should automatically react by flexing or moving its leg if it is at all conscious.

Ear reflex
Touch or gently flick the tip of the ear flap with one finger. If a cat is at all conscious, it should automatically react by twitching its ears.

FIRST AID WARNING
A semiconscious cat may feel a stimulus and be unable to react if it is in shock. Never persist with an examination longer than needed.

COLLAPSE AND SHOCK

Recognizing shock
A cat may go into a state of shock following a serious accident. It will feel cold to the touch, and its breathing and pulse will be rapid.

Conserve heat *(left)*
Make the cat as comfortable as possible. Keep it warm (unless it is suffering from heatstroke) by wrapping it loosely in a blanket or towel. Do not constrict the cat's breathing.

EMERGENCY ACTION
Do not let an unconscious cat lie on one side for more than 5–10 minutes. Do not give an unconscious cat anything by mouth.

Recovery position
If a cat is unconscious or having difficulty breathing, place it on its side with the head tilted downward. Open the mouth and ensure that the airway is clear.

159

ACCIDENTS

The most important thing to do in the event of an accident is to contact a vet as soon as possible. Even if a cat appears to have no external injuries, it should be given a checkup, since there may be internal damage. A vet or trained assistant can advise on immediate first aid measures. If time is critical, ask someone to telephone the clinic and alert the vet that you are on the way.

Accidental falls
A cat is unlikely to injure itself if it falls from a tree, but injuries do occur with falls from greater heights. All windows should have screens to prevent your cat from accidentally falling.

MOVING AN UNCONSCIOUS CAT

1 Move the injured cat out of any danger area. A blanket or coat will serve as an improvised stretcher. Lay the blanket out flat and then gently ease the cat onto it.

2 With the help of an assistant, gently lift the blanket up, taking care not to let the cat slip off. If the cat is conscious, you may need someone to restrain it.

3 Ensure that the airway is clear by removing any fluid from the mouth and pulling the tongue forward *(see page 158)*. Stop any severe bleeding by covering the wound with a pressure bandage or gauze pad *(see page 170)*.

4 It is advisable to transport an injured cat in a secure container. An unconscious cat can be lowered on the blanket into a large box so as not to disturb it.

MOVING AN UNCOOPERATIVE CAT

1 An injured cat will be frightened and perhaps in pain. Talk to the cat to reassure it, approaching it very slowly and cautiously. A frightened cat may be aggressive and defensive, even to people it knows.

2 Cover the cat with a blanket to restrain it and to prevent it from running off. It may be advisable to wear gloves to protect your hands.

Make sure paws are enclosed

3 With one hand holding the scruff of the neck, wrap the blanket quickly but securely around the cat's body, leaving the head exposed *(see page 129)*.

4 Maintaining a firm grip on the cat's scruff, pick the cat up and put it into a carrier for transportation to the vet. Do not release your hold until you are about to fasten the carrier.

FRACTURED LIMBS

Lifting an injured cat
If you suspect that a cat has a fractured limb, handle it very carefully. Lay it on a blanket and pick it up, keeping the injured limb uppermost. Avoid twisting or bending its body. Put the cat in a carrier and get it quickly to a vet.

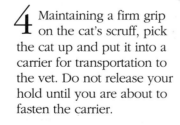

FIRST AID WARNING

Transport and handle a cat with a fractured limb so as to cause it the minimum disturbance. Do not attempt to apply a splint yourself, since this will distress an injured cat and probably do more harm than good.

RESUSCITATION

Prompt action taken in an emergency situation, such as a traffic accident *(see pages 160–161)*, may save your cat's life. Fortunately, emergencies are rare, but they usually occur without warning and allow little or no time to get professional help. If a cat is unconscious and its breathing and heartbeat have stopped, get someone to telephone the vet for you in order to obtain immediate advice while you try to save the animal's life.

Resuscitation must be carried out following the guidelines given opposite (or by a vet), to ensure that a cat has the best chance of recovery. A cat may suffer respiratory and heart failure following drowning, electric shock, or poisoning. For the cat to survive, its breathing or heart must be restarted within a few minutes.

ARTIFICIAL RESPIRATION

The mouth should be open to ease breathing

1 Remove the cat's collar. Lay the cat on one side in the recovery position *(see page 159)*. Open the mouth and clear the airway of any fluid *(see page 158)*.

2 If the cat has stopped breathing but the heart is still beating, proceed with artificial respiration. Using a towel, pull the tongue forward to clear the throat. This may stimulate breathing, causing the cat to regain consciousness.

3 If the cat remains unconscious, place your hands on the chest and apply gentle pressure. This expels air from the lungs, allowing them to be refilled with fresh air. Repeat every five seconds until the cat breathes.

CARDIAC MASSAGE

If a cat is unconscious and there is no sign of a heartbeat or breathing, direct stimulation of the heart may be attempted. Place your fingers on the chest at the point of the elbow and press down gently but firmly. Repeat five or six times at one-second intervals. Alternate with artificial respiration for up to ten minutes, after which the procedure is unlikely to be successful.

MOUTH-TO-MOUTH RESUSCITATION

1 If the chest cavity has been damaged, the lungs may not refill automatically, and you will have to blow air into them. Hold the unconscious cat in an upright position with its mouth closed.

2 Breathe into the nostrils for two to three seconds to inflate the lungs. The movement of the chest will be clearly visible. Pause for a two-second rest, then repeat.

Support the cat's body

3 Continue with resuscitation until the cat starts to breathe on its own. An alternative method involves breathing simultaneously into the cat's nose and open mouth.

FIRST AID WARNING

The resuscitation methods described here should only be attempted if a cat is unconscious and does not respond to normal stimuli. Do not use an excessive amount of force, since this can injure the cat.

DROWNING

1 Most cats dislike going too near water, but accidents do happen – for example, a kitten may fall into a pond or a swimming pool.

2 Take the cat out of the water and dry it quickly with a towel. If the cat is motionless, drain any water from the lungs. Hold the cat upside down by firmly gripping its hind legs above the ankle joints.

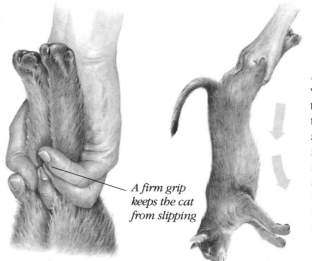

A firm grip keeps the cat from slipping

3 Swing the cat vigorously (but not violently) downward to remove water from the lungs. If there are still no signs of the cat resuming breathing, resuscitation should be started *(see opposite)*. Get the cat into warm surroundings as soon as possible.

CHOKING AND FOREIGN BODIES

Professional help from a vet is essential if a cat is having any difficulty with its breathing. However, in the unlikely event of a foreign body becoming lodged in your cat's throat, you may not have time to call a vet. You will need to take emergency action. A cat with an object such as a fish-bone lodged in its throat will be distressed and make convulsive choking noises and may paw at its mouth. This should not be confused with a cat that is coughing up a hairball.

CHOKING

1 If the cat is making coughing and choking noises and gasping for air, try to look at the back of the throat. Get someone to contact a vet for advice, meanwhile restrain the cat and open its mouth *(see page 130)* to identify the object. As with all first aid treatments, keep the cat as calm and still as possible.

FIRST AID WARNING

Do not put your fingers in a cat's mouth if it is choking, since you are likely to get bitten. It .will help if the cat is restrained by being wrapped in a towel *(see page 129)*.

---

2 Locate the object with a flashlight. Try to remove the object with tweezers or the handle of a teaspoon. If this does not work, try to dislodge the object by turning the cat upside down.

FOREIGN BODY IN THE MOUTH

1 A carelessly discarded fish hook can occasionally become lodged in a cat's mouth. If the hook is superficial, the barb can be carefully cut off with pliers or wire cutters.

2 The remains of the hook can then be removed safely. Do not pull on a fishing line or thread that has been swallowed. Consult a vet immediately to locate and remove the hook or needle.

FOREIGN BODY IN THE EYES

1 Grass seeds and tiny pieces of grit are the most common objects to become lodged in a cat's eyes. Hold the eyelids open and examine the eye carefully. If something has penetrated the eyeball, do not touch it.

2 If the foreign body is loose or under the eyelid, you may be able to float it out with eye drops or one or two drops of olive oil. If you are in any doubt, contact a vet.

OTHER FOREIGN BODIES

Foreign body in the ears
Similar techniques to those above can be used to remove objects such as grass seeds, from just inside the ear. Float out seeds using ear drops or one or two drops of olive oil.

FIRST AID WARNING

Never poke tweezers or anything else into a cat's ears or eyes. A great deal of damage is done this way by well-meaning owners who do more harm than good. Remember: if in doubt, it is always best to call in a vet.

Foreign body in the paws
Grass seeds and burrs can become stuck in the fur between the toes, or a cat can get a splinter in its paw. If a cat cannot remove the object with its teeth, it may need to be dislodged by hand or using tweezers. Do not try to remove any object that is embedded in the paw pad. It is advisable to consult a vet if the injury is more than a superficial scratch.

POISONING

Poisoning is not a common occurrence, since cats are extremely careful feeders and also vomit very readily if they have eaten anything harmful. However, a cat may ingest a poison accidentally by eating either plants that have been treated with insecticides or poisoned prey. If a cat's coat becomes contaminated with chemicals, it will lick them off in an attempt to clean itself. Two common household poisons are slug killer and painkillers such as aspirin.

POISONS

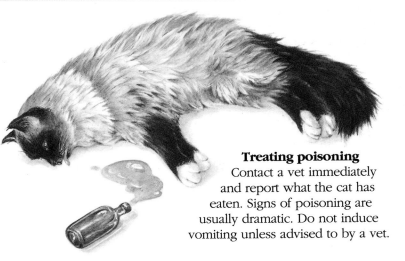

Treating poisoning
Contact a vet immediately and report what the cat has eaten. Signs of poisoning are usually dramatic. Do not induce vomiting unless advised to by a vet.

COAT CONTAMINATION

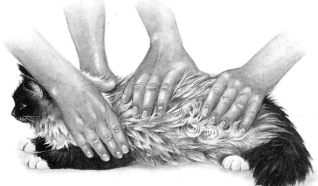

1 Soften paint or tar with petroleum jelly to help with removal. It is essential to remove any contaminant from the coat immediately to prevent the cat from licking it off while grooming.

2 Cut away any heavily contaminated fur, taking care not to cut the cat's skin. Antifreeze, bleach, and disinfectant can all be fatal if ingested.

FIRST AID WARNING

Never use solvents or paint stripper to remove paint from a cat's coat, since these are very toxic. A cat with a badly contaminated coat needs veterinary treatment. If possible, take a sample of the contaminant with you when you visit the clinic.

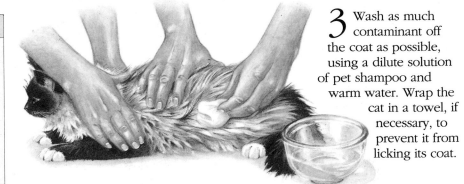

3 Wash as much contaminant off the coat as possible, using a dilute solution of pet shampoo and warm water. Wrap the cat in a towel, if necessary, to prevent it from licking its coat.

COMMON POISONS IN THE HOME

Poisonous plants
Many plants are toxic to cats. Most felines enjoy chewing on greenery but usually prefer grass to the leaves of plants. A cat may occasionally develop a taste for a particular plant and will need to be discouraged from eating it.

Poinsettia

Christmas cherry

Spotted dumb cane

Sweet pea

Clematis

Azalea

Oleander

Delphinium

Rhododendron

Lupin

Christmas rose

HOUSEHOLD POISONS

Poison	Signs of poisoning	Action
Rodent poisons (e.g. arsenic, strychnine, thallium, warfarin)	Restlessness, abdominal pain, vomiting, bleeding, and diarrhea. Potentially fatal.	Consult a vet immediately. Antidotes to some types of poison are available.
Antifreeze	Lack of coordination, vomiting, convulsions, followed by coma. Potentially fatal.	Consult a vet immediately. An injection may block the effect.
Alcohol, methylated spirits	Depression, vomiting, collapse, dehydration, and coma. Potentially fatal.	Consult a vet immediately. Note what type of poison has been eaten.
Painkillers (e.g. aspirin, disprin, paracetamol)	Lack of coordination, loss of balance, and vomiting. The gums will be blue if a cat has swallowed paracetamol. Potentially fatal.	Consult a vet immediately, who will induce the cat to vomit. Painkillers intended for humans are toxic to cats.
Disinfectants, household cleaners (e.g. phenols)	Severe vomiting, diarrhea, nervous signs, staggering, and coma. Potentially fatal.	Consult a vet immediately. Note what type of poison has been eaten.
Insecticides and pesticides (e.g. chlorinated hydrocarbons)	Muscle twitching, drooling, convulsions (sometimes triggered by handling), and coma. Potentially fatal.	Consult a vet immediately. There is no specific antidote.
Slug and snail poisons (e.g. metaldehyde, baysol)	Continuous salivation, muscle twitching, vomiting, diarrhea, lack of coordination, convulsions, and coma. Potentially fatal.	Consult a vet immediately. Treatment is often effective if given promptly.

BITES AND STINGS

When a cat is allowed to go outdoors, fights with other felines over territory are likely. Cat bites can quickly become infected and form abscesses, which require veterinary treatment. Insect bites and stings are rare, but can cause considerable pain and distress. In tropical countries, venomous snakes, spiders, scorpions, and toads are other hazards. Cats are usually more inquisitive than aggressive toward these creatures, but they can get too close. Kittens play-hunting are especially likely to get bitten.

INSECT BITES AND VENOM

Bee and wasp stings
Sudden swelling and pain result from stings around the face or feet. Urgent veterinary treatment is essential if a cat is unsteady or disoriented or has trouble with its breathing.

Treating stings (right)
A bee sting, which looks like a splinter in a red, swollen area, can be removed with tweezers. Bathe with a weak solution of sodium bicarbonate. An ice pack will help reduce swelling.

Snake and spider bites
Try to identify the type of creature that has bitten the cat, since this will help with the treatment. A snake bite will be visible as two deep puncture wounds, and the cat will keep licking the affected area.

Treating bites (right)
Slow the spread of the venom by applying a cold compress and then a pressure bandage just above the bite (see page 170). Contact a vet immediately.

Toad venom
Some species of toad secrete a venom on their skin. If a cat picks up a toad, this venom causes the cat's mouth to become painful and inflamed.

Treating toad venom (left)
If the cat will allow it, flush out the mouth immediately with clean water, being careful to prevent the cat from inhaling any fluid. Wipe away excess saliva and keep the cat quiet. Seek veterinary help.

CAT BITE ABSCESS

1 When a cat bite is not detected at the time it happens, it is likely to become septic. After a few days, it will be swollen and very tender. If the cat will allow it, clean the area around the abscess and clip away surrounding fur.

2 Bathe the swollen area with lukewarm water or a weak salt solution (one teaspoonful in a glass of water). Frequent bathing should bring the abscess to a "head." Do not try to lance the abscess yourself.

Expel any remaining pus once the abscess has burst

3 After bathing for 24 hours, the abscess should burst, producing foul-smelling pus. Once the pressure has eased, the cat will feel much better.

4 Keep the wound clean and continue bathing so that the abscess does not re-form. The cat may need antibiotics to control infection.

FIGHT WOUNDS

Occasionally a cat may return home in a very disheveled state, signifying that it has been in a fight. Some of its fur may be missing, ears and eyelids may be torn, and teeth or claws broken. Any minor cuts or lacerations should be cleaned up *(see page 170)*. A bite from another cat is not normally visible at the time. In many cases, this turns septic in a few days and the wound becomes swollen and painful to the touch. If you know that your cat has been in a fight and if it seems to be distressed, it is best to take it to a vet for a thorough examination.

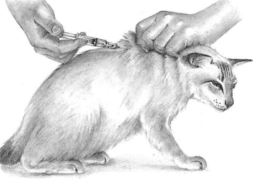

Ears may be torn and bleeding

Neck may be bitten

Base of the tail is a common site for abscesses

EMERGENCY ACTION

Call a vet immediately if an abscess is very large or does not rupture 24 hours after bathing. The abscess may need to be lanced and drained by a vet. Antibiotics may sometimes be required to prevent the abscess from re-forming and to eliminate bacterial infection.

Assessing an injury

Examine the cat to determine its condition. Stop any bleeding and consult a vet if an injury is serious.

BANDAGING WOUNDS

Since most cats lead quite adventurous lives, they risk an occasional injury. The most common causes of wounds are bites and scratches from other cats *(see page 169)*. If your cat is injured, the main first aid aim is to control shock and minimize blood loss. The best way to stop bleeding is to cover the wound with a gauze pad and apply pressure. A handkerchief or strips of cloth can be used as a bandage in an emergency.

CUTS AND LACERATIONS

1 Examine the cat, keeping it as calm as possible. Gently wipe away any blood or dirt, using a damp cotton ball. Contact a vet if the injury is more than superficial.

2 With the help of an assistant to steady the cat, trim away any matted fur. Petroleum jelly applied around the edges of the injury will prevent hair from falling into the open wound.

3 Minor cuts and lacerations can be treated with a mild antiseptic suitable for cats, such as dilute hydrogen peroxide solution.

STOPPING BLEEDING

Apply a cold-water compress

1 Contact a vet at once if an injury is bleeding heavily. Meanwhile stanch the flow of blood with a gauze pad soaked in cold water.

2 The bleeding should stop after a minute or two. If it does not, secure the gauze with a bandage and put another pad over the top.

3 Wrap another bandage around the cat to keep the gauze pads in place. Maintain pressure on the bleeding points. Consult a vet.

APPLYING DRESSINGS

1 Simple dressings can be applied to minor wounds or to control bleeding, but bandaging of more serious injuries should be done by a vet. First cover the wound with a gauze pad.

2 Secure the gauze pad over the wound by covering with bandages. The bandage should be firm but not too tight, since this may restrict the circulation. Do not apply a tourniquet without veterinary advice.

SERIOUS INJURIES

Torso wounds

When there are very extensive injuries or bruising, a complete body bandage can be made out of a clean pillow case, in order to reduce further injury on the way to the vet. All dressings should be changed daily, or when there is evidence of blood or discharge seeping through.

BANDAGING A MINOR WOUND

FIRST AID WARNING

Never bandage a limb too tightly, since this may constrict the circulation. Do not move a limb if there is pain or swelling, since bones may be broken.

1 When bandaging a paw, first clean the site of the wound *(see opposite)*. Put small tufts of cotton between the cat's toes to prevent rubbing and discomfort.

Insert cotton between the toes

2 Cover the wound with an absorbent pad ½ in (1 cm) thick. Do not use cotton, since the fibers may stick to the wound and disturb any clot that is forming.

3 Secure the pad in position with adhesive tape, looped under the foot, then around the leg. Be careful not to restrict the blood supply. Check the wound regularly to make sure that it is healing.

BURNS AND OTHER INJURIES

Even though cats are always getting into inaccessible places, they usually manage to avoid being burned or scalded. Their thick coats may also give them some added protection. When accidents do occur, they are usually caused by boiling water, hot grease, or open fires. Shock is associated with burns and cold-related injuries, so it is vital to consult a vet at once.

SCALDS

1 If a cat has been scalded, the affected area of its body must be swabbed with cold water as soon as possible. Do not apply any butter or skin cream to the wound.

Swab wound with cold water

2 Make an ice pack with ice cubes in a freezer bag or wrapped in a piece of clean cloth. Apply this to the burn while contacting the vet.

3 Apply petroleum jelly to the wound (if the cat will allow it). Do not cut away any surrounding fur. Do not cover the wound.

CHEMICAL BURNS

1 Wash any chemical off the coat at once. Weak solutions of sodium bicarbonate or vinegar may help neutralize the effects of acid and alkali, respectively.

Use only water where chemical is unknown

2 Put an ice pack on the injured area while contacting the vet. An affected limb can be placed under cold running water for several minutes. It may be advisable to wear rubber gloves when touching any chemicals.

ELECTRICAL BURNS AND SHOCK

1 Kittens are most likely to chew or bite through electrical wiring. Even if a cat only suffers mild burns to the tongue and to the corners of its mouth, it needs to be examined by a vet, since there may be other injuries or complications.

2 Switch off the current before touching the injured cat. If this is not possible, use a broom handle to move the live wire away from the cat. Contact a vet.

SUNBURN

Apply sunblock cream to ears

Sunburn on the ear tips
Cats in hot, tropical regions are prone to sunburn on their ears. As a precaution, cats with pale-colored coats should be kept indoors during the sunniest part of the day and their ears protected with a sunblock cream.

EMERGENCY ACTION

Severe electrical shock can be fatal or result in heart failure. The cat may require emergency resuscitation (*see pages 162–163*). Contact your vet immediately for further advice.

FROSTBITE AND HYPOTHERMIA

Frostbite
The parts of a cat's body that can be affected by frostbite in severe weather are the paws, tail, and ears. Paws can be gently warmed by immersing in warm water.

Hypothermia
This involves a cooling down of the whole body and can result in death. The cat should be placed in a warm, sheltered place and covered with blankets. Warm the cat up gradually.

OTHER EMERGENCIES

Even though most cats have no trouble giving birth, problems do sometimes occur. You should contact a vet if your cat seems to be distressed or in pain, or has been straining for more than half an hour without producing a kitten. A mother cat and newborn kittens may occasionally need immediate first aid while a vet is on the way or if veterinary help is not available. This may mean the difference between life and death. Other emergencies needing urgent first aid treatment include heatstroke and asphyxia.

LABOR PROBLEMS

When to call a vet
Keep a close but discreet watch on your cat as she goes into labor. If she seems distressed and has not delivered a kitten within 30 minutes after she has started straining, you should contact a vet.

QUEENING PROBLEMS

Disorder	Description and signs	Action
Miscarriage	Premature labor is rare in cats but can be caused by an accident, infection, stress, or an abnormal fetus. Symptoms may include straining, vomiting, diarrhea, and bleeding from the vulva.	If you know the kittens are not due, contact a vet immediately. Keep the cat warm and quiet. There is not much that can be done to prevent miscarriage once it begins.
Uterine rupture	This may occur as the result of an accident in late pregnancy, or just before or during the delivery. The queen may show signs of shock or abdominal discomfort, or she may fail to go into labor. If the queen is in shock, she may collapse, breathe rapidly, and have a racing pulse and diluted pupils.	Contact a vet immediately. Shock requires urgent veterinary treatment. Keep the cat warm and calm, reassuring it by gently speaking to it until it can be treated by a vet.
Vulval discharge and hemorrhage	Some vulval discharge is normal for a few days after the birth, but if it is brown or foul-smelling, it may indicate an infection or retained fetal membranes. Bleeding from the vulva signifies internal hemorrhage and can be life-threatening.	Consult a vet immediately. Keep the queen warm and quiet to prevent her from going into shock. Put a pad of gauze against the vulva to soak up any discharge or blood.
Fading Kitten Syndrome	Sometimes kittens may be born underweight or deformed or fail to suckle. In some cases, apparently normal kittens will fade away and die after a few days or weeks.	There is often not much that can be done to save affected kittens, although you may be able to feed them by hand. Severely deformed kittens may need to be humanely destroyed by a vet.
Rejected kittens	Occasionally, a queen may not be able to produce sufficient milk or be unable to nurse her litter. She may reject the kittens shortly after the birth, or the runt of the litter may be ousted by its siblings. Like many animals, a cat produces several offspring to allow for some not surviving to adulthood in the wild. Rejected kittens may be fostered by another queen or reared by hand (see page 151).	Consult a vet for advice. Orphan kittens must be kept warm, well fed, and clean. To begin with, they must be fed every two hours with special replacement cat milk. After feeding, the anal area of a kitten needs to be gently wiped with a piece of damp cotton to encourage elimination of waste products. The mother cat may accept the kittens back when they are partially weaned.

HELPING WITH QUEENING

1 If a kitten is stuck partly out of the vulva and the queen seems to be in difficulty, you need to act immediately. Wash your hands, then lubricate the vulva with petroleum jelly. Firmly grasp the kitten and gently ease it out as the queen bears down.

2 If the queen ignores the kitten, you must pull off the membrane covering it and clear its mouth and nostrils of mucus. Rub it dry with a towel. When it is breathing, soak some cotton and scissors in antiseptic. Tie the cotton around the umbilical cord about 1 in (2.5 cm) from the navel.

3 Cut the umbilical cord on the side attached to the placenta. Alternatively the cord can be separated by hand. Do not pull on the cord, since this may damage the kitten. Encourage the kitten to suckle.

FIRST AID WARNING

If a kitten's head or one of its limbs is held up inside the birth passage, do not attempt to force it out. Seek veterinary help immediately.

HEATSTROKE AND ASPHYXIA

Heatstroke
A cat suffering from heatstroke may collapse. Lower its temperature by wrapping it in towels soaked in cool (but not ice-cold) water.

Asphyxia
A cat may collapse if it inhales carbon monoxide fumes. It must be allowed to breathe fresh air as soon as possible and encouraged to move about to stimulate circulation.

Chapter 10
SHOWING

BREEDERS WHO exhibit pedigree cats at shows are striving to achieve perfection within the standards of their chosen breed. Competition among entrants to have their feline judged to be the best of a breed or best in a category is always intense. The formalities for entering a cat in a competition and the ways in which different types of cat show are organized vary around the world. Shows often have classes for household pets, and this is probably a good place for a beginner to start. The competitive drive of showing your cat can become totally absorbing, so be warned!

CAT SHOWS

Breeders constantly strive to produce the finest cats for exhibition, so visiting a show can be a rewarding and educational experience. Almost every familiar breed is likely to be present at a large cat show, as well as a few rare ones not generally seen. Shows are run by the controlling authority for all cat clubs and societies in a particular country. In the United States, the Cat Fanciers' Association (CFA) and other cat organizations establish breed standards, register pedigrees, and approve the dates of major shows. In Great Britain, the Governing Council of the Cat Fancy (GCCF) is responsible for the show rules and has approved standards for all the pedigree cat breeds.

THE HISTORY OF CAT SHOWS

First pedigree breeder
An early North American breeder, Mrs. Clinton Locke, pictured with her two Siamese cats.

The first modern cat show *(below)*
Crystal Palace in London was the venue for the first large cat show, which took place in 1871. Longhairs and British Shorthairs were among the cats exhibited. The first North American cat show was held in New England for the Maine Coon breed at about the same time.

HOW A SHOW IS ORGANIZED

Kitten class
Cats under nine months of age have separate open classes for all breeds. Kittens compete with others of the same breed, sex, and color. At a large show, kitten classes for popular breeds may be divided by sex or by age.

Open class
The most important of all the classes. At a large cat show there will be open classes for all the breeds represented. To become a champion, a cat must win three open classes at different shows.

Neuter class
Pedigree cats that are castrated males or spayed females have separate open classes of their own. They compete against other neuters of the same breed and are judged according to the same breed standards as intact cats.

Household pet class
Neutered cats of unknown or unregistered parentage can be entered in the class for household pets. There is no written standard for nonpedigree cats. They are judged for their uniqueness, any unusual markings, and temperament.

BRITISH AND AMERICAN SHOWS

Shows in Great Britain
All cat shows operate under the Governing Council of the Cat Fancy. After a veterinary inspection, cats are given a number. Pens are numbered but carry no other distinguishing marks. Judging takes place on a table that is wheeled from pen to pen (see page 183).

Shows in the United States
The Cat Fanciers' Association is the largest of the eight cat authorities in the United States. Classes are divided into "allbreed" or "specialty," with a separate household pet competition. Judging takes place on tables set up in full view of the public attending the show.

JUDGING SHOW CATS

Over the past century, interest in pedigree cats has played a central role in creating the rich spectrum of breeds we see today. Selective breeding programs have been used to enhance particular physical characteristics and to create cats that look attractive to the human eye. Fortunately, in contrast to dog breeding,

there have been few instances of this having harmful effects. A pedigree cat is judged against a standard that specifies how a perfect example of its type should look. Points are awarded for the appearance of the cat's head, eyes, body, and coat.

Registering a kitten
Register your pedigree kitten with the appropriate cat association.

EXAMPLES OF HOW CATS ARE JUDGED

Head (20 points)
Round face, with full cheeks and a strong chin.

Body (25 points)
"Cobby" type, low on legs, with a broad, deep chest.

Tail (10 points)
Thick and of medium length.

British Blue Shorthair (left)
The British Shorthair is a compact and powerful cat, with a strong, muscular body on short legs. It has a broad head, with round eyes, and ears set well apart.

Eyes (10 points)
Copper, orange, or deep gold in color.

Coat (35 points)
Short and dense (not too long or fluffy). Color should be light to medium blue, with no tabby markings or silver tipping.

Tail (10 points)
Short and bushy, but in proportion to body length.

Head (25 points)
Round and broad, with a short nose and a strong chin.

Eyes (10 points)
Deep orange or brilliant copper.

Cream Shaded Cameo Longhair (right)
This classic Pedigree Longhair cat has a "cobby" build, with a sturdy, rounded body and short, thick legs. It has a broad head, with round eyes and small ears.

Coat (40 points)
Long and thick, and fine in texture. Color should be white with cream tipping, with no tabby markings.

Body (15 points)
Stocky or "cobby" in build, with short, thick legs.

Head (20 points)
Wedge-shaped face, long and narrow, with pricked ears.

Eyes (20 points)
Clear, bright, vivid blue. A squint is a fault.

Tail (5 points)
Long and tapering, with no kink at the end.

Red-point Siamese (left)
The Siamese has a unique, pale-colored coat and darker markings on its face, paws, and tail. It has a long, slim, oriental build, with slanted eyes, and elegant legs and feet.

Body (20 points)
Long, svelte, oriental build, with slim legs.

Coat (35 Points)
Very short and fine. Color should be white, shading to apricot on the body and reddish-gold on the points (barring is permissible).

Head (15 points)
Round and gently wedge-shaped, with large, preferably tufted, ears.

Usual Abyssinian (right)
The Abyssinian's ticked coat, in which each hair has several different-colored bands, is very distinctive. The build of this cat is muscular and lithe, and the head is less elongated than that of the Siamese.

Eyes (10 points)
Amber, hazel, or green. A light eye color is undesirable.

Coat (45 points)
Short, fine, and close-lying, with double or preferably treble ticking. Color should be a ruddy brown ticked with black. A pale overall color is a fault and so are black or gray base hairs.

Body (30 points)
Medium in length, and lithe and muscular in appearance. A "cobby" build is not permissible.

Head (20 points)
Medium, wedge-shaped head, with a distinct nose break.

Eyes (25 points)
Golden-yellow eyes preferred. Green eyes are a serious fault in Brown Burmese, but Blue Burmese may show a slight fading of color.

Coat (20 points)
Short and glossy, with a satin finish. Color should be a mixture of blue and cream, with no obvious barring.

Body (35 points)
Medium in size, feeling muscular and heavier than it appears.

Blue Tortoiseshell Burmese (left)
The Burmese cat is prized for its smooth and glossy coat. Its build is more round-bodied and muscular than that of the Siamese. The British Burmese is more oriental in appearance than the sturdier North American variety.

TAKING PART IN A CAT SHOW

The preparations for showing your cat should begin several weeks, or even months, beforehand. If your cat has not been shown before, you will have to get it accustomed to being confined in a pen and to being handled. Maintaining a show cat involves good feeding and daily grooming.

GROOMING FOR SHOWING

A cat's eyes and ears must be spotlessly clean

1 A longhaired cat needs to be bathed before a show to ensure that its coat is in perfect condition *(see pages 76–77)*. On the show day, remove any staining around the eyes with a damp cotton ball.

2 Final grooming takes place in the pen. Carefully brush the shorter hairs on the cat's face with a small toothbrush. Do not put the toothbrush too close to the eyes.

3 As a finishing touch, use a slicker brush to make the cat's fur stand out fully from its body. The fur around the cat's neck should frame the face.

SHOWING EQUIPMENT
The only items allowed in a cat's pen are a litter box, blanket, and water bowl. You will also require the following: cat food; a white ribbon or elastic collar on which the cat's entry number can be pinned; vaccination certificates; show documentation; and brushes and combs.

Litter box

Blanket

Feeding bowl   *Water bowl*

Slicker brush   *Toothbrush*

THE DAY OF THE SHOW

Examining *(left)*
Any cat entered for competition should be in good health. In some countries every cat entered is examined by a vet. A sick animal is not allowed to take part in the competition.

A cat is scrutinized by a judge

Awarding points *(below)*
A pedigree cat is judged against its breed standard. A maximum of 100 points is awarded for its head, eyes, condition, and coat *(see pages 180–181).*

Judging *(right)*
Cats are judged at a movable table near their pens. In North American shows, cats are examined in public.

Prizewinning cat
A well-trained show cat sits proudly in its pen and enjoys all the attention that it receives. Rosettes are pinned on the pens of the winners.

Best in show *(below)*
The climax of a cat show comes when all the entries have been judged. This is when the best cat in the show is announced.

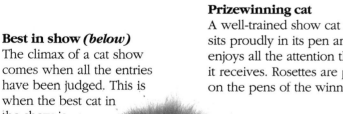

GLOSSARY

Abscess Collection of pus forming painful swelling. Usually the result of a cat bite.
Ailurophile Cat lover.
Ailurophobe Cat hater.
Albino Lack of pigment melanin, causing white fur and pink eyes.
Angora Breed of cat with long hair and slim, long body. Lacks woolly undercoat of true longhaired cats.
Awn hairs Bristly hairs of undercoat with thickened tips.

Back-cross Offspring of mating between adult cat and its own kitten.
Bicolor Coats consisting of white hair mixed with one other color.
Breed A type of cat, named for its color, size, and shape.
Breed standard A description of ideal characteristics against which each breed of cat is measured. This is determined by the national cat society of each country.

Calico American name for Tortoiseshell-and-White cat.
Canker *See* Otitis.
Carpal pad Extra fleshy pad above others on front paws, thought to help stop skidding when a cat lands after jumping.
Castrate To remove testicles to prevent reproduction and sexual behavior.
Cat flap Hinged flap set in a door that enables a cat to come and go as it wants.
Cat flu *See* Feline respiratory disease.
Catnip The herb *Nepeta cataria*, which gives off a scent that most cats find irresistible. Used in some cat toys.
Cattery Establishment that boards cats while owners are away.
Chinchilla Longhaired cat whose white fur is tipped with black.
Chlamydial disease Affects cat's eyes and the respiratory system.
Chromosomes Tiny strands of DNA that store genetic information.
Cobby A stocky, rounded body shape, with short legs and long fur.
Coccidiosis Caused by protozoan parasite that affects the digestive system.
Colorpoint A cat whose face, ears, legs, feet, and tail are of a different color than the rest of its body.
Conjunctivitis Inflammation of the thin outer layer of the eye, causing watering and soreness. Associated with Feline respiratory disease.

Dermatitis An inflammation of the skin.
Dew claw Extra toe on hind leg above paw. Its function is not known.
DNA Chemical substance that makes up chromosomes, from which all life begins.
Dominant gene The gene that overrides a recessive gene in a pairing of chromosomes, so that its characteristics are always evident in the offspring.
Down hairs Soft hairs under guard hairs that insulate body.

Ear mites Tiny parasites living in ear canal, causing irritation.
Elizabethan collar Cardboard or plastic funnel fitted over head to prevent cat interfering with wounds.
Estrus Periods during which a female cat is sexually responsive to a male, commonly known as heat or season.

Feline Calici Virus (FCV) One of the two common viruses causing Feline respiratory disease. Signs include coughing, sneezing, watery eyes, and runny nose. *See also* Feline respiratory disease and Feline Viral Rhinotracheitis.
Feline Dysautonomia Nervous disorder causing persistent pupil dilation, regurgitation, and rapid weight loss. Once known as Key-Gaskell Syndrome.
Feline Infectious Anaemia Disease caused by parasite in blood. Signs are fever, weight loss, and lethargy.
Feline Immunodeficiency Virus (FIV) A relative of the HIV virus, which weakens the immune system, eventually causing death. Highly contagious to other cats, but not to humans or other animals.
Feline Infectious Enteritis (FIE) Virus causing loss of white blood cells, and fatal in most cases. Signs include depression, severe diarrhea, vomiting, and abdominal pain. Also called Feline Panleukopenia.
Feline Infectious Peritonitis (FIP) Usually fatal virus disease. Signs include fluid accumulation in the abdomen, jaundice, and anemia.
Feline Leukemia Virus (FeLV) Virus affecting lymphatic system, suppressing immunity to disease. Usually fatal. Signs include weight loss, vomiting, diarrhea, and difficulty in breathing.
Feline Panleukopenia *See* Feline Infectious Enteritis.
Feline respiratory disease Sometimes known as "cat flu". *See* Feline Viral Rhinotracheitis and Feline Calici Virus.
Feline Urological Syndrome (FUS) Inflammation of bladder and urethra. Sandy deposits in bladder and urethra can lead to blood in urine and difficulty in urination. Obstruction is a real emergency.
Feline Viral Rhinotracheitis (FVR) The more serious of the two common viruses that cause Feline respiratory disease. Signs include high fever, and a discharge from the eyes and nose. May sometimes be fatal, especially in kittens and elderly cats. *See also* Feline respiratory disease and Feline Calici Virus.
Feral Domestic animals that have reverted to a wild state.
Flea collar Special collar with chemical impregnated to kill fleas.
Fleas The most common parasite found on a cat's skin. Live by feeding on blood. Cats may be sensitive to bites or flea dirt.
Flehming Grimacing and lifting the upper lip to bring a scent into contact with the Jacobson's organ for sensory analysis. Usually related to sexual behavior of tomcats.
Flukes Parasites found in intestine and liver, causing diarrhea and anemia.
Foreign Another term for a cat of oriental appearance, such as a Siamese cat.

Gastritis Inflammation of the stomach walls causing vomiting and lack of appetite.
Gene Tiny bead of DNA on chromosomes that carries information on physical characteristics such as coat color, eye color, length of coat, and many others.
Gene pool The total number of genes available within a breed.
Glaucoma Enlargement of eyeball caused by increased pressure from within.
Groom To brush or comb a cat's coat.

Guard hairs Thick, coarse hairs that protect softer down hairs underneath, in some cats providing a waterproof layer.

Hematoma Blood blister in ear flap usually due to scratching and bursting of a blood vessel.

Harvest mites Parasites that appear in the autumn and can cause skin irritation. Also known as chiggers.

Haw *See* Third eyelid.

Heat *See* Estrus.

Heartworms Parasite found in tropical areas of the world. Transmitted by mosquitoes and lives in heart.

Hock A cat's ankle.

Hookworms Bloodsucking worms that live in small intestine. Can cause weight loss, diarrhea, and anemia.

Intact An unneutered cat.

Jacobson's organ A sensory organ above the roof of the mouth that analyzes smells and tastes, and sends a signal to the brain.

Keratitis Inflammation of cornea, resulting in eye becoming cloudy.

Key-Gaskell Syndrome *See* Feline Dysautonomia.

Kitten pen Wire cage in which a new cat or kitten can live briefly while being introduced to a household.

Lactational Tetany Due to inadequate calcium levels in blood during nursing. Causes vomiting and staggering. Also known as Milk Fever.

Lice Parasites that suck blood, causing anemia in a severe infestation.

Litter The absorbent granules used in a cat's toilet box. Also a family of kittens.

Litter box Shallow box filled with litter.

Longhaired Cat whose coat has long top hairs, with a thick, woolly undercoat.

Mange mite Minute parasites that burrow into a cat's skin, causing chronic hair loss, irritation, and inflammation.

Manx Tailless breed of cat, caused by mutant gene that can be associated with lethal characteristics.

Mastitis Infection of milk glands.

Metacarpal pads Thick pads of tissue on paws to keep a cat from slipping.

Middle ear disease Infection of inner ear. Signs include tilting of head to one side, staggering, and partial deafness.

Milk Fever *See* Lactational Tetany.

Neuter To castrate males or spay females to prevent reproduction and unwanted sexual behavior.

Nictitating membrane *See* Third eyelid.

Odd-eyed Cat with one blue eye and the other orange. Blue eyes in white cats may be associated with deafness.

Oriental Foreign breeds with almond-shaped eyes, wedge-shaped heads, and long limbs. Examples are the Abyssinian, Siamese, and Burmese.

Otitis A term for inflammation of outer ear, caused by mites, bacteria, or foreign bodies. Also known as canker.

Pedigree A record of ancestry, showing a cat's family tree over several generations.

Pedigree Longhair Pedigree cat with a long outer coat. Also known as Persian.

Peritonitis An inflammation of the peritoneum in the abdomen. *See also* Feline Infectious Peritonitis.

Persian *See* Pedigree Longhair.

Points The face, ears, legs, feet, and tail, which may be a different color than the rest of the body, as in a Siamese cat.

Polydactyly Having extra number of toes.

Prolapse Condition in which internal organs such as uterus or rectum are pushed outside body by straining.

Quarantine Period of isolation in which animals entering certain countries from abroad must be kept to prevent the spread of rabies.

Queen Unspayed female cat.

Queening Giving birth.

Rabies Serious virus disease affecting nervous system. Transmission is by bite from an infected animal.

Recessive gene One whose characteristics are overridden by a dominant gene in each pairing of chromosomes, so that it is not evident in the resulting offspring.

Register List of pedigree cats. In order to be allowed to enter cat shows, each purebred cat must be registered upon birth with the national cat authority.

Ringworm Form of fungal infection that causes scaly skin and irritation.

Roundworms Parasites found in cat's digestive tract, feeding on digesting food. Can cause diarrhea, especially in kittens.

Scent marking A cat marks its territory with urine, or with scent from glands on the head, sending a clear message to any intruding cats. It may also scratch furniture and trees, sharpening its claws and leaving a scent from glands on its paw pads.

Scratching post A covered post upon which a cat can exercise its claws without damaging furniture. It will also mark the post with scent to denote its territory.

Scratching *See* Scent marking.

Season *See* Estrus.

Selective breeding Breeding of pedigree cats by planned matings to enhance certain physical characteristics, such as eye color.

Siamese Oriental, shorthaired cat, with pale-colored coat and points of a different color.

Spay Operation to remove ovaries and uterus to prevent estrus and pregnancy.

Stud Uncastrated tomcat used specifically for breeding purposes.

Tabby Cat with striped, blotched, or spotted markings. Pattern used in the wild for breaking up the body shape so that the cat can hide itself in the undergrowth.

Tapeworms Intestinal parasites that feed on cat's partly digested food. Fleas are needed to complete the life cycle.

Territory Area patrolled by a cat, which it considers to be its own. A cat will fiercely defend its territory against intruders.

Third eyelid Eyelid that is sometimes visible at corners of a cat's eyes.

Ticks Parasites that burrow into a cat's skin to feed on blood. Some types of tick can transmit diseases.

Tipped Coat whose top hairs are tipped with a different color than the undercoat.

Tomcat An uncastrated male cat.

Topcoat Outer layer of hair that forms overall color of cat.

Tortoiseshell Coat resulting from linkage of dominant and recessive orange genes, both carried by female chromosome. Tortoiseshell cats are usually female.

Toxoplasmosis Disease caused by parasite, often in raw meat, which affects digestive system. Causes diarrhea. Can sometimes be transmitted to humans.

Tumor Swelling on or beneath skin due to abnormal growth. Can be cancerous.

Undercoat Thick layer of insulating fur under topcoat.

Vetting in Examination by a vet upon entry into a British cat show. No longer required in American cat shows.

Weaning Gradual change in a kitten's diet from mother's milk to solid food.

Zoonoses Diseases that can be passed between vertebrate species including man.

CAT CARE RECORD

Cat's name: ....

Breed: ....

Pedigree name: ....

Names and breeds of parents: ....

....

Date of birth: ....

Sex: ....

Color of coat: ....

Color of eyes: ....

Favorite foods: ....

VETERINARY RECORD

Name and address of veterinarian: ....

....

....

Telephone number: ....

Emergency telephone number: ....

Medical history (any recent illnesses with dates of

visits to the vet): ....

....

....

....

VACCINATIONS

Date of first vaccination: ....

Date annual booster due: ....

Other vaccinations: ....

....

BREEDING RECORD

Name and address of stud breeder: ....

....

....

Telephone number: ....

Birth date of litter: ....

Names and sexes of kittens: ....

....

....

BOARDING

Name and address of cattery: ....

....

....

Telephone number: ....

Name and address of cat sitter: ....

....

....

Telephone number: ....

ADDITIONAL INFORMATION

USEFUL ADDRESSES

American Cat Fanciers' Association
PO Box 203,
Point Lookout, Missouri 65726
Cat registry; sponsors cat clubs
throughout the country and
internationally.

American Society for the Prevention of Cruelty to Animals (ASPCA)
441 East 92nd Street,
New York, New York 10028
Nonprofit animal advocacy group;
America's oldest humane society.
Educational information, publications,
audiovisual materials, legislative
support and activities nationwide,
behavior hotline for NYC area.

American Veterinary Medical Association
1931 North Meacham Road,
Schaumburg, Illinois 60173

Canadian Cat Association
83 Kennedy Road South,
Unit 1805,
Brampton, Ontario
Canada L6W 3P3

Cat Fanciers' Association
1805 Atlantic Avenue,
Manasquan, New Jersey 08736
The largest cat registry in North America.
Sponsors cat shows
throughout the country and
internationally. Produces educational
information and audiovisual materials.

International Cat Association
PO Box 2684,
Harlingen, Texas 78551
Cat registry; sponsors cat clubs around
the United States and internationally.

Cat Fancier's Federation
9509 Montgomery Road,
Cincinnati, Ohio 45242
Cat Registry; sponsors cat shows.

Humane Society of the United States
2100 L Street, NW,
Washington, DC 20037
Nonprofit animal advocacy organization.
Publications, specialty items, audiovisual
materials, and legislative and
investigative activity.

PERIODICALS

Cat Fancy
PO Box 6050,
Mission Viejo, California 92690

Cats Magazine
PO Box 290037,
Port Orange, Florida 32129

I Love Cats
950 Third Avenue, 16th Floor,
New York, New York 10022

FURTHER READING

Anderson, Robert, & Wrede, Barbara,
Caring for Older Cats & Dogs,
Williamson Pub. Co., 1990
Behrend, Katrin & Wegler, Monica,
How to Raise a Happy & Healthy Cat,
Barron's, 1991
Caras, Roger, *The Cat Is Watching,*
Simon & Schuster, 1990
Caras, Roger, *A Celebration of Cats,*
Simon & Schuster, 1987
Fogle, Bruce, *Know Your Cat,* Dorling
Kindersley Inc., 1991
Gerstenfeld, Sheldon, *The Cat Care
Book,* Addison Wesley, 1990
Hawcroft, Tim, *The Howell Book of
Cat Care,* Howell Book House, 1991
Martyn, Elizabeth, & Taylor, David,
The Little Cat Behavior Book, Dorling
Kindersley Inc., 1991
Martyn, Elizabeth, & Taylor, David,
The Little Cat Care Book, Dorling
Kindersley Inc., 1991
Morris, Desmond, *Catwatching,*
Crown, 1987
Taylor, David, *The Ultimate Cat Book,*
Simon & Schuster, 1989
Thies, Dagmar, *Cat Care,* T.F.H.
Publications, 1989
Viner, Bradley, *The Cat Care Manual,*
Barron's, 1986

INDEX

ACKNOWLEDGMENTS

Author's acknowledgments

Any work of this kind requires an enormous effort from a large number of people. All of these deserve my sincere gratitude. The team at Dorling Kindersley is unsurpassed. In the forefront of this admirable group are Project Editor Alison Melvin, Art Editor Lee Griffiths, and Managing Editor Krystyna Mayer. It is these tireless people who create the book. The author is only one of the team. The photographs produced by Dorling Kindersley set the highest standards. Steve Gorton and Tim Ridley approached the notoriously difficult task of capturing cats in every pose with humanity, immense skill, and inextinguishable good humor.

My former colleagues at the Waltham Centre for Pet Nutrition, especially Dr. Helen Nott, Dr. Jo Wills, Dr. Ivan Burger, Dr. Kay Earle, Helen Munday, and Dr. Ian Robinson have been most helpful, as have Pedigree Petfoods, the Pedigree Education Centre, and Denise Reed. Many veterinarians and the BSAVA have given help and encouragement, particularly Dr. Bruce Fogle. The Royal Veterinary College, my own *alma mater*, was very helpful. I am grateful to the Principal, Professor Lance Lanyon, and the staff of the Queen Mother Hospital and its Director, Professor Roger Batt. Polly Curds and Liz Ravenor of the RVC Animal Care Trust provided much cheerfully given assistance. Professor Oswald Jarrett and Dr. Helen Laird of Glasgow University Veterinary School kindly sent information on feline viruses.

Among the countless individuals who I must thank are Betty Thomas and Sophie Hamilton-Moore of the Feline Advisory Bureau, Peter Neville, everyone at the Wood Green Animal Shelter, and Benita Horder, librarian at the Royal College of Veterinary Surgeons.

Publisher's acknowledgments

For providing animals for photography: Ben and Vicky Adams *(Ferret)*; Rosemary Alger *(Champion Typha Plush Velvat, also known as "The Toy Boy")*; Stacey Berenson *(Tammy)*; Jenny Berry *(Hamster and Puffin)*; Maria Dorey *(Bella)*; Moyra Flynn *(Sydney, Bianca, Bill, and Ben)*; Janice Hall *(Seamus)*; Pat Heller *(Phoebe)*; Intellectual Animals *(Jules, Wilma, Cherry, and Glynis)*; Sue Kempster *(Harry and Melissa)*; Krystyna Mayer *(Mruczek)*; Alison Melvin *(Nelson and Winston)*; Christina Oates *(Cloud)*; Eunice Paterson *(Soames and Fleur)*; Sally Powell *(Violet)*; Sue Roberts *(Blue Boy and Hoppy)*; Pauline Rogers *(Misty, Lulu, and Ollie)*; Di Sanderson *(Billy)*; Celia Slack *(Bluey and kittens)*; Katy Slack *(Chockie and kittens)*; Karen Tanner *(Cherami, Fortune Cookie, and kittens)*; Hazel Taylor *(Maisie)*; Amanda Topp *(Tiddles)*; Alison Trehorne *(Lollipop and Humbug)*; RVC Animal Care Trust *(Chloe)*; Beany Smith *(Smudge)*.

For modeling: "Cookie" Baran and Stacey Berenson.
For handling cats: Kate Forey, Jenny Berry, Etta Rumsey, and Di Sanderson.
For supplying equipment and materials: Animal Fair, Kensington, London W8.

For design assistance: Colette Cheng.
For editorial assistance: Lynn Parr.
For page make-up and computer assistance: Patrizio Semproni.
For picture research: Diana Morris.

Dorling Kindersley wish to thank Terence C. Bate BVSc, LLB, MRCVS of the RSPCA for his valuable advice on the text.

ASPCA acknowledgments

Numerous staff provided special assistance, helping to research and review material for this publication, most especially Gordon Robinson, VMD, Micky Niego, Jacque Schultz, and Liz Teal.

Illustrations

Angelica Elsebach: 157, 158–159, 160–161, 162–163, 164–165, 166, 168–169, 170–171, 172–173, 174–175
Chris Forsey: 13, 45, 47, 51, 98, 99, 100, 102, 104, 106, 108, 109, 110, 112, 114, 116, 118, 120, 122, 124

Photography

KEY: t *top*, b *bottom*, c *center*, l *left*, r *right*
All photography by Steve Gorton and Tim Ridley except for:
Animals Unlimited: 46bl, 70t, 71bl, 179bl
Ardea: 13c
Bodleian Library, Oxford: 12t
Jane Burton: 5tl, 8tl, 10, 16t, 17r, 18t, 18b, 19cr, 21cr, 25b 27b, 34c, 36r, 42b, 44c, 44b, 46t, 56t, 58t, 71br, 78–79, 80–81, 82–83, 84–85, 86–87, 98b, 100t, 105bl, 110b, 114t, 119b, 120t, 121b, 124t, 125b, 133cl, 143bl, 154b, 179tl
Bruce Coleman Ltd: 13tr, 44t Hans Reinhard
Eric Crichton: 167cl, 167cr, 167brc
Tom Dobbie: 167t
E.T. Archive: 12br
John Glover: 167crc, 167blc
Jerry Harpur: 167clc, 167bl, 167br
Marc Henrie: 101b
Michael Holford: 12c, 12bl
Larry Johnson: 179br
Dave King: 7tr, 9b, 11cl, 11b, 19cl, 21t, 22–23, 26t, 26c, 27t, 70b, 71t, 71c, 88, 89t, 89c, 92–93, 94, 133bl, 143t, 143c, 143br, 154c, 179c, 180c, 180b, 181
Oxford Scientific Films: 13tl Frank Schneidemeyer, 50b London Scientific Films
David Ward: 134b
Matthew Ward: 130t, 131, 133cr, 133br